BATTLE HEROES

VOICES FROM AFGHANISTAN

BATTLE HEROES
VOICES FROM AFGHANISTAN

By Allan Zullo

SCHOLASTIC INC.

In memory of Sergeant Schuyler Patch, 25,
a member of the Illinois Army National Guard, who,
while serving with the Thirty-third Infantry Brigade
Combat Team, was killed on February 24, 2009,
in Kandahar, Afghanistan, by a roadside bomb.
–A.Z.

ISBN 978-0-545-81810-0

Copyright   2010 by The Wordsellers, Inc.

12 11 10 9 8 7 6 5 4 3   15 16 17 18 19 20/0

Printed in the U.S.A.   40
First Scholastic printing, January 2015

Acknowledgments

I wish to thank the heroes featured in this book for their willingness to relive in personal interviews with me the dramatic and sometimes emotional memories of their combat experiences.

I also want to thank the following persons for their cooperation: Adrien F. C. Starks, Chief, Civic Outreach Team, Office of the Assistant Secretary of Defense, Public Affairs/Community Relations; Evelyn Jutte, Public Affairs Officer, Office of the Chief, Army Reserve, Army Reserve Communications; and Dewey Mitchell, Chief of Public Affairs, Brooke Army Medical Center.

Author's Note

After my book *War Heroes: Voices from Iraq* was published in 2009, I felt a duty to write about another band of warriors—the courageous members of the United States Army, Navy, Air Force, and Marines who have been waging a valiant fight in Afghanistan.

Since October 2001, they have risked life and limb to carry out their missions in a deadly world of roadside bombs, ambushes, and suicidal terrorists. And these brave Americans also have been willing to lay down their lives for their comrades.

Every one of them is a hero.

I wish I could write about all their personal stories of valor, honor, and sacrifice. But, of course, that's not possible. Instead, I have written ten stories that reflect the countless breathtaking acts of heroism that have occurred, and continue to occur, every day in the war in Afghanistan.

The heroes spotlighted in this book represent some of the tens of thousands of American troops who, with steadfast boldness, have been battling a ruthless enemy in knee-deep snow of rugged mountains, in scorching temperatures of sand-blasted desert plains, and in deadly close combat of militant-occupied villages.

All the heroes featured in the following pages earned top military medals and come from different branches of the military, from career Marines to Army Reserve soldiers. One Green Beret received the Distinguished Service Cross, given to a member of the U.S. Army for remarkable bravery, extraordinary heroism, and sacrifice in battle against an enemy of the United States. Several received the Silver Star, which is given to a person in any branch of the armed services who displays exceptional courage and gallantry in action. Others in the book were awarded the Bronze Star.

For this book, I reviewed battle accounts and military citations. Then I conducted personal, lengthy interviews with the selected heroes and asked them to relive the heart-stopping moments that earned them their medals for valor. Some found it easy to recall their experiences. Others found it difficult and emotional because one or more of their comrades had been killed in battle. As most combat veterans will tell you, the highest duty in war is to protect the buddy on your left and the buddy on your right.

All persons profiled in this book shared a common trait— humility. None viewed themselves as heroes; all said they were just doing the job they were trained to do and were no different from their comrades. At the ceremony where he received the Distinguished Service Cross, Master Sergeant Brendan O'Connor said, "I've never been more honored, but this medal belongs to my whole team. Every member was watching out for the other, inspiring each other, and for some, sacrificing for each other. We all fought hard, and it could just as easily be any one of them standing up here getting this medal. Every one of them is a hero."

O'Connor was a member of a team that became the most decorated Special Forces unit for a single battle in the war in Afghanistan. There were so many heroes in the two-day fight that this book features two stories about them—one spotlighting O'Connor and the other focusing on his valiant fellow soldiers.

When you read the gripping accounts of the gutsy actions of all the heroes in this book, you'll see that they displayed a tenacity that spurred them to reach far beyond their personal limits. Some found within themselves an incredible courage that they didn't even know they had.

Their stories are written as factual and truthful versions of their recollections, although some of the dialogue has been re-created.

Because there are so many military terms used in these accounts, there is a glossary at the back of the book. Also, certain places and the complete names of a few of the heroes' comrades are not given for security reasons.

Some of what you'll read is a little graphic. Although these passages might be hard to stomach, there was no attempt to soften them because that is how they really happened.

Regardless how you feel about this or any war, Americans in uniform deserve our respect, our support, and our gratitude. This book is a salute to their courage, honor, and gallantry.

— Allan Zullo

Contents

BATTLE HEROES

Voices from AFGHANISTAN

Operation Enduring Freedom

On September 11, 2001 — the day that changed the world — nearly 3,000 innocent people were killed in the most devastating terrorist attack ever on American soil.

In a coordinated assault, 19 suicidal terrorists hijacked four commercial jetliners. They deliberately crashed two of the planes into New York City's World Trade Center, leveling its twin 110-story towers. Another plane slammed into the Pentagon, damaging the headquarters of the Department of Defense. Before the fourth plane could reach its target — possibly the White House — it crashed into a field in Shanksville, Pennsylvania, after passengers fought the terrorists for control of the aircraft.

The United States quickly determined that the perpetrators were from the Islamic militant organization al-Qaeda, headed by Osama bin Laden. He and his fellow fanatics were based in Afghanistan, where they had set up a network of camps to train radicals to carry out terrorism in other parts of the world.

Afghanistan is a poverty-stricken, landlocked nation about the size of Texas located in south-central Asia between Iran and Pakistan. Nearly all of its 31 million people are Muslims who follow Islamic religious codes and traditional tribal and ethnic practices. The vast majority live in small tribal compounds in the country's massive mountain ranges and remote valleys in the north and east, and on the barren desertlike plains of the south and west.

At the time of the 9/11 attacks, Afghanistan was under the control of the Taliban — a fundamentalist Islamic militia that had seized power in 1996. Because of their extreme interpretation of Islamic law, they banned most leisure activities and entertainment such as music, dancing, picnics, television, and sports. Also forbidden were children's toys, including dolls and kites; card and board games; cameras and photographs. The Taliban enforced harsh penalties for reading novels, magazines, and newspapers. They beat adult men for grooming their beards and women for making noise when they walked. Women were forbidden to attend school or hold jobs other than in the health-care field. People accused of even minor infractions were whipped by canes. For more serious offenses, the Taliban chopped off hands and held public hangings and stonings at soccer fields. Brainwashing and propaganda were used to fuel people's hatred of the Western world.

The Taliban also played host to bin Laden and his al-Qaeda radicals, granting them full protection in Afghanistan's desolate mountains. The terrorists thought they were safe from America's military might. They were dead wrong.

Nine days after the 9/11 attacks, the United States demanded that the Taliban turn over all the leaders of al-Qaeda, immediately close every terrorist training camp, and round up all the country's terrorists and their supporters. The Taliban refused.

So on October 7, 2001, the United States and several allies (called coalition forces) launched Operation Enduring Freedom and invaded Afghanistan. Within three months, coalition forces — spearheaded by the U.S. Army, Navy, Air Force, and Marines — toppled the Taliban government, destroyed al-Qaeda training camps, and drove most of the militants into the jagged mountains bordering Pakistan. Although many of al-Qaeda's top leaders were dead or captured, bin Laden managed to escape and, from a secret location, urged terrorists around the world to attack Western countries.

Despite the early successes by coalition forces, the fighting in Afghanistan continued, partly because military resources were diverted to Iraq after it was invaded by the United States in 2003. Nevertheless, on October 9, 2004, Afghans held their first direct democratic elections, including voting for a president. The following year, they elected their parliament.

Throughout this war, the United States has poured billions of dollars in aid into Afghanistan. Much of the money has gone to build schools, mosques, roads, bridges, hospitals, clinics, water-treatment plants, and dams, and to train the Afghan National Police (ANP) and Afghan National Army (ANA). But progress to secure the future of Afghanistan and eliminate the militants there has been slow, frustrating, and violent.

The Taliban — supported by outside terrorist groups and Afghan drug lords — have proven to be tough enemies that still wield powerful influence in various regions of the country. Since 2006, they have increased attacks on coalition forces with roadside and suicide bombings, ambushes, and direct assaults by trained and well-equipped militants.

Afghanistan's military, police, and elected government officials haven't been strong enough to quash the insurgents and create a new and safe society. The country continues to rely on the help of American-led coalition forces. By the summer of 2010, the American troop level was expected to reach nearly 100,000 for Operation Enduring Freedom. Most U.S. forces have been fighting in eastern and southern Afghanistan along the Pakistan border. The rest make up part of a second operation, known as the International Security Assistance Force (ISAF), under the command of the North Atlantic Treaty Organization (NATO). Joining the Americans are about 68,000 troops from 42 countries.

The ongoing mission of the U.S. military has come at a price: 945 American troops killed and another 2,779 seriously wounded as of January 2010, the beginning of the ninth year of the war.

Although there has always been some disagreement about the handling of the war in Afghanistan, there's one issue that everyone can agree on: The men and women of the U.S. military have served with unbelievable courage, compassion, and commitment.

The Stand

CAPTAIN JASON AMERINE

Captain Jason Amerine had just sat down to dinner at a restaurant when his cell phone rang. It was Dan Petithory, his senior communications sergeant, with shocking news: "Two planes have flown into the World Trade Center," Petithory announced, his voice quaking. "Our nation is under attack!"

Amerine and his fellow Green Berets were far from home — in the eastern European republic of Kazakhstan, training Kazakh paratroopers. Rushing back to his base, the Special Forces officer didn't have time to deal with his emotions. As the team leader, his mind was whirring with questions: *Where will my men and I be deployed? And when? What should we be doing to prepare ourselves?*

Watching the heart-wrenching video of the collapse of the Twin Towers and the raging fire at the Pentagon from the terrorist attacks, Amerine seethed with anger. "This means war," he told his team sergeant, Jefferson "J.D." Davis. "I don't exactly know where, but I think it'll be in Afghanistan, because it's a pretty good bet that Osama bin Laden and al-Qaeda are behind the attacks."

Within weeks, the 30-year-old West Point graduate headed up Texas 12 (spoken as "Texas One Two"), the code name for Operational Detachment Alpha 574 of the Army's Third Battalion, Fifth Special Forces Group (Airborne). The small force of ten Green Berets and an air force combat controller was given a crucial — and difficult — mission: Help Afghan freedom fighters overthrow the tyrannical Taliban regime and destroy the al-Qaeda camps so the fanatics no longer would have a safe haven to recruit and train a new generation of extremists.

It was the first step in Operation Enduring Freedom's challenge to dismantle the terrorist network responsible for the 9/11 attacks and to assist the Afghans in forming a *loya jirga*, or grand council of tribal leaders, for the creation of a new legitimate government.

For Amerine, this was a task he was meant to do. Ever since he was 14, he had dreamed of joining the Army Special Forces. Now here he was, ready to lead his team in the most dangerous mission of their lives. What Texas 12 lacked in size, it made up for in guts, skill, and advanced training in unconventional warfare.

In late October 2001, days after anti-Taliban commander Abdul Haq was assassinated, Amerine and his fellow Green Berets sneaked into Oruzgan Province by helicopter. At a secret location, they met Hamid Karzai, one of several leaders of the Pashtuns, the country's ethnic majority. The soft-spoken, English-speaking chief had been living in exile in nearby Pakistan. Karzai said he wanted to help ignite a revolt against the Taliban. American military and intelligence officials considered Karzai an unimportant political figure with no real power. But Amerine and his men believed that Karzai could play a major role in the overthrow of the Taliban. Despite the doubts of the military brass, the Green Berets teamed up with Karzai in the push to oust the Taliban.

Karzai explained that the key to controlling the province was capturing its capital, Tarin Kowt, in the same region that spawned the Taliban's rise to power. "Tarin Kowt represents the Taliban's heart," he told Amerine. "Crush that heart, and we kill the Taliban."

"But the Taliban there seem to have a lot of followers," the captain said.

"Just because a village appears to support the Taliban, that doesn't mean the people are pro-Taliban," Karzai explained. "A lot of these villages simply align themselves with the Taliban out of fear that if they don't, the Taliban will come and wipe them out and hurt and kill their families."

On November 15, Amerine arranged for the U.S. military to bring in weapons, ammunition, and other supplies — an operation known as a lethal-aid drop — so he could start arming and training a force of Afghan freedom fighters. Hundreds of anti-Taliban Afghans took the weapons, but instead of joining Amerine, they returned to their homes to defend their villages against further Taliban harassment. The captain discovered a harsh truth: Although many people supported Karzai, they weren't ready to fight alongside him and the Americans, because Karzai hadn't proven himself yet.

The next day brought unexpected good news. The people in Tarin Kowt had rebelled against the local Taliban government, hanged the mayor from a lamppost, and chased the rest of his supporters out of town.

"The Taliban will try to retake Tarin Kowt," Karzai told Amerine. "They'll be looking for revenge, to punish everyone and turn it into a bloodbath. We need to leave immediately for Tarin Kowt. We must do whatever we can to defend the town."

"We'll definitely be outnumbered big-time, and the odds will be stacked against us," said the captain. "But we have something the Taliban doesn't — air support."

Because the Green Berets had no vehicles of their own, Amerine rounded up what basic transportation was available. The vehicles included pickups, flatbed trucks, two touring vans, and several battered United Nations SUVs. Then he, his team, and 30 untrained Afghan freedom fighters drove all day and into the night. One of his soldiers rode on the roof of a truck to protect sensitive communications equipment.

When the small force arrived in Tarin Kowt, nobody in the streets greeted the men, and the few people Amerine saw seemed grim and quiet. Karzai met with senior Pashtun tribal leaders from the area. Later, at their invitation, the captain joined them in a special meal honoring the first day of Ramadan — a month-long Islamic religious observance in which Muslims fast between sunrise and sunset. Amerine had eaten only a few bites when he was told in a matter-of-fact manner that a huge convoy carrying hundreds of Taliban fighters had left the city of Kandahar, the Taliban's spiritual center, for Tarin Kowt.

Amerine's mind began racing. *We have eleven Americans and a bunch of highly motivated, but untested, Afghans going up against a massive number of Taliban fighters who are angry and determined to retake the town. How are we going to defend it? If we have to retreat, how will we leave? How can we keep Karzai alive?*

"Well, it was nice meeting all of you," he told the gathering. "I must leave now and organize a defense of this town."

But the Pashtuns insisted that he stay and enjoy the meat, rice, naan (a form of bread), and tea as they broke the fast. After all, they said, the Taliban wouldn't arrive until daybreak. Knowing he had to prepare for battle, he simply couldn't sit any longer and excused himself.

On his way out, the captain told Karzai, "Get me every able-bodied fighter you can. Once I get a big enough force, we'll set up a defense outside of town and direct air strikes on the convoy."

Amerine told his men what they were about to face. Like true Green Berets, they went into combat-preparation mode. His weapons sergeant analyzed the maps. His air combat controller alerted the air force and navy of the need for air support — fast. His communications sergeant contacted headquarters, letting them know about the impending attack. Others checked their equipment and weapons. Throughout the night, Master Sergeant "J.D." Davis made sure that everyone was staying on task.

Since their deployment, the Green Berets hadn't fired a shot in the war. Many members of his team had experienced combat before, but not in Afghanistan. Amerine had hoped to say something profound to mark the occasion, but all that came out of his mouth was, "Let's smoke 'em!"

Shortly before sunrise, the Americans and a few dozen Afghan fighters piled into pickups, vans, and cars. They drove about five miles to a plateau and fanned out along a ridge that overlooked a valley. At one end of the valley was a narrow mountain pass, through which the captain expected the Taliban convoy would enter.

"This is the perfect spot for us to defend the town," Amerine told his men. "From here, we have great visibility. We'll bomb them as they come through the pass and try to bottle them up before they can reach the town." His men organized the freedom fighters into a basic defense. *We don't have enough people to really defend against a large attack*, Amerine thought. *But maybe we can stop the enemy with our aircraft.*

He assumed the Afghans were willing to fight, but they were untested and spoke little English. Some had never even fired their new weapons. The Taliban, on the other hand, were well trained and well armed. *Well, I have to work with what I have.*

The Green Berets pulled out laser equipment, set up radio communications, and scanned the area with high-tech binoculars for the first sign of the Taliban. Just as the sun started to rise, the captain and his soldiers saw a cloud of dust billowing at the entrance to the pass. "Right on cue," Amerine said.

Emerging from the swirling dust, the first wave of Taliban vehicles roared into the valley. Amerine peered through his binoculars and saw that about 500 Taliban militants were crammed into extended cab pickups and big SUVs, armed with Kalashnikov automatic rifles, machine guns, and rocket-propelled grenades (RPGs). Larger trucks outfitted with artillery and antiaircraft guns soon rolled into view.

"We have a lot of bad guys coming our way," the captain said.

Staff Sergeant Alan Yoshida, the air-combat controller, radioed the pilots of three air force F-16 fighter jets circling above. At 30,000 feet, the jets were so high that no one on the ground could see them. "Troops in contact," Yoshida told the pilots, meaning friendly forces were engaging the enemy. Turning to Amerine, he said, "Are we clear to engage?"

"Cleared hot," Amerine replied, the military term for permission to drop bombs.

Sergeant First Class Daniel Petithory used a sophisticated laser range finder to calculate the distance to the initial targets. The device was plugged into a handheld GPS that gave him precise coordinates, which were relayed to the pilots.

Unfortunately, the first laser-guided bomb missed. But the second and third bombs destroyed the convoy's lead vehicles. Amerine smiled with satisfaction when he watched the trucks burst into fireballs. *We just might win this battle*, he thought.

As bombs continued exploding, Taliban vehicles scattered like cockroaches, but still kept advancing. Then, through the loud noise, Amerine heard men shouting behind him and engines cranking up. He turned around and saw the Afghan freedom fighters sprinting to their vehicles and driving away. Frightened by the sheer number of Taliban fighters and unnerved by the chaos of combat, they were trying to flee to the relative safety of Tarin Kowt.

They're panicking! Amerine thought. *They don't realize how devastating our air strikes are.* "Hey, get back here!" he shouted.

He ordered the Afghans to stay, but even if they could understand English — and most couldn't — they were not returning. Some of the Americans were yelling "Stop! Stop!" and ran in front of the trucks, trying to prevent them from leaving. But there was no halting the terror-stricken Afghans. For every vehicle the Green Berets stopped, two or three others would squeal past them. The Americans commandeered a couple of trucks and maneuvered them in an attempt to block the remaining vehicles, but without success. *This is so frustrating*, the captain thought. *We're pulling defeat from the jaws of victory.*

Amerine knew that seeing the local freedom fighters retreat at the first sign of combat would shatter any confidence the people of Tarin Kowt had in Karzai and the Americans. He also knew that he couldn't continue the battle without his men having vehicles ready to quickly move as the battle progressed. *It would be suicide if we were stranded here*, he thought.

Reluctantly, the captain ordered his men into the remaining vehicles and withdrew the entire force. As the speeding Afghan trucks hurtled toward town, bouncing and swerving along the potholed road, the Green Berets in the pickup beds were nearly tossed out.

Amerine had been on an emotional roller coaster ever since he arrived in Tarin Kowt. He had first felt it would be a difficult challenge for his small group to repel the overwhelming larger Taliban force. But when his team set up on the ridge and the bombs started dropping, he figured there was a good chance of winning. Now the Afghans were running away for the shelter of Karzai's headquarters.

When he reached Tarin Kowt, Amerine told Karzai what had

happened on the ridge. Karzai shook his head in disappointment and then asked, "What do you need?"

"I need to take the vehicles back out there and continue the bombing to protect this town," Amerine replied. "Hamid, I need you to gather all the men you can muster who can fire a weapon and are willing to fight. Send as many as you can as fast as you can to catch up with us."

"Okay, go, go, go!"

The Americans seized the vehicles and zoomed off. On the way, they received reports from the pilots overhead that the Taliban had broken through the pass and overrun the observation point that the team had been forced to abandon.

The Green Berets took up a new position on the outskirts of town as their "no-penetration line."

"If the Taliban get past us, we lose the town," the captain told his team. "All the aircraft in the world won't help us, because we can't bomb the town to save it. So if the Taliban break through our line in large numbers, the fight is lost, and we're going to have to grab Karzai and get him out of here." Looking into the determined eyes of his men, he vowed, "But we're not going to let any of that happen."

Everyone on the team sprang into action, either firing their weapons or directing aircraft. Watching another 2,000-pound bomb incinerate a group of enemy trucks, Amerine gloated, "Okay, we're back in the game!"

Eleven Americans and three fighter jets were battling the 500-man-strong Taliban . . . and winning.

The captain's soaring spirits, however, took a nosedive when the pilots reported that they had run out of bombs and needed to return to base. Despite the battering that the Taliban convoy was taking, the surviving trucks were still rumbling toward Tarin Kowt. Before the planes left the area, the pilots swooped down and, courageously ignoring Taliban shoulder-launched anti-aircraft missiles, strafed the vehicles until the ammo was spent.

When the planes departed, the enemy drew nearer, but the valiant Americans fought them off. *We have to stand our ground or else the people here will be slaughtered*, Amerine thought. Soon navy F-14 fighter jets arrived on the scene and started a new round of bombing.

Inspired by the courage and never-say-die attitude of the Americans, a growing number of armed Afghans began showing up. They indicated they wanted to fight, so Davis, the team sergeant, organized them in a second line of defense on another side of town.

Meanwhile, women, children, and the elderly were trickling toward the Americans, cheering them on and clapping after every bomb exploded. Children were pointing, laughing, and snooping around the troops' rucksacks. A couple of Afghans asked for their trucks back. *This is crazy*, Amerine thought. *It's turning into a circus atmosphere — and we're in the middle of a battle!* Some of his men moved the crowd back and urged parents to take their children home where it was safer.

After several hours of close combat and countless air strikes, the Americans had demolished the enemy. An estimated 300 Taliban fighters lay dead amid the smoldering wreckage of dozens of vehicles.

Just when Amerine thought victory was assured, he received word that about two dozen Taliban fighters coming from another direction were attempting to blast their way through at a spot being defended by the local Afghans. Following Davis's lead and guidance, the Afghans not only beat back the enemy but captured some prisoners.

Those who surrendered admitted they had been ordered by Taliban leaders to make an example of Tarin Kowt's rebellious citizens by murdering them and leaving their bodies in the street.

Finally, late in the morning, the battle ended. The remaining Taliban fighters had turned and fled back into the mountains. The pilots, however, weren't through and continued to harass the retreating force all the way back to Kandahar. At one point, a pilot radioed to Amerine, "I see an enemy target. . . . They think I can't see them. . . . Take that!" After a distinct blast was heard over the radio, the pilot reported, "Okay, they're gone."

Amerine and his fellow Green Berets had saved Tarin Kowt. With some assistance from the untrained Afghans, they had made a courageous stand and won a stunning victory against an experienced force that outnumbered them by more than ten to one. The Americans had earned the respect and trust of the Afghans, who celebrated throughout the day. Karzai's prestige soared.

The Green Berets couldn't relax yet because they had to prepare for an anticipated second attack. They took positions on a hill for the night and kept aircraft overhead for reconnaissance. But the Taliban had been so rattled by their humiliating defeat that they made no further attempt to recapture Tarin Kowt.

When Amerine returned to the town, Karzai told him, "The local religious leaders came last night and told me that they'd all be dead if it hadn't been for the Americans. I am grateful to you and your team."

"It was a big win that went beyond the battle itself," Amerine said. "This victory will build your credibility and convince more of your countrymen to turn against the Taliban."

Amerine was right. Over the next two weeks, Karzai convinced an increasing number of tribal leaders to join his side. In dozens of villages, big and small, people tore down the white Taliban flag and raised the green, white, and black national flag of Afghanistan to show their support for his cause. (The colors have since changed to green, black, and red.) As he gained stature, Karzai negotiated several Taliban surrenders and began the work of creating a new temporary government.

Meanwhile, Amerine's team and fighter jets attacked Taliban convoys that tried to move out of Kandahar, preventing the enemy from recapturing any lost territory.

Given 300 disciplined but fairly inexperienced Afghan freedom fighters by Karzai, the Green Berets headed toward Kandahar, engaging in firefights along the way. Davis used these battles to toughen and train Karzai's men, who were gaining confidence a little bit day by day. "As long as they see us smiling and not panicking during combat, it will keep them focused on the mission," Amerine told his team.

On December 3, after a pitched street-by-street battle, the Green Berets and freedom fighters captured the town of Shawali Kowt, but could not gain control of a vital bridge over the Arghandab River, the gateway to Kandahar.

That night, Taliban forces launched a major counterattack, triggering a retreat by the Afghans. Over the next eight hours, despite being outnumbered two to one and in grave danger of being overrun, the Americans fought back hard. Yoshida, the air-combat controller, orchestrated numerous air strikes from AC-130 gunships, thwarting the Taliban charge and forcing the enemy to retreat.

The following day, as the Afghans scaled to the top of a ridge overlooking the Taliban-controlled town of Sayyd Alma Kalay, they were hit by machine-gun fire and RPGs. The Afghans began retreating, so Amerine and his men charged up the hill and fired down on the enemy. The Americans' actions spurred the Afghans to rejoin the fight. Despite being exposed to intense fire, Yoshida advanced toward the hilltop and directed air strikes that wiped out three enemy positions. Amerine's team finally drove off the Taliban and took control of the town and bridge while Karzai's men held the ridge.

As combat eased, the leaders from battalion headquarters arrived by helicopter on December 5 to give Amerine and his men a break. For the first time in weeks, the Green Berets received care packages and letters from home.

Taking a breather on the hill that they had just taken, the men read their mail and enjoyed the treats that had been sent to them. About 100 yards away, Amerine met with Karzai, who was using a concrete building as his temporary headquarters. "The Taliban plan to formally surrender," Karzai told him. "I'm expecting a delegation from Kandahar later today to discuss the terms. It looks like I'm going to be the interim leader of Afghanistan."

"That's great news, Hamid."

"My country and I are indebted to you and all the Americans who helped defeat the Taliban. Hopefully, our national nightmare is nearing an end."

"But in the meantime, we're still at war."

Amerine left the headquarters and walked over to a staff officer from the battalion to discuss plans for continued air strikes. They were studying a map when, out of nowhere, a thunderous explosion rocked the hill, pitching Amerine high into the air. He tumbled head over heels and landed so hard he was briefly knocked out. When he came to, he felt a searing pain in his leg. A piece of hot shrapnel had ripped open his thigh. Everywhere he looked he saw mangled, bloody bodies and people running and yelling. Everything sounded weird and was muted by the swish of rushing air. He realized then that his eardrums had burst from the blast.

Some soldiers were shouting that they were under attack, but Amerine knew the Taliban didn't have a weapon that powerful. "We were hit by friendly fire," he explained, trying to calm those around him. "It was one of *our* bombs."

Despite the stabbing pain in his thigh, Amerine joined others who weren't seriously injured and tended to those who were. The number of casualties was staggering: three Americans and ten Afghans killed; another forty American and Afghan soldiers wounded. Even Karzai, the future leader of Afghanistan, didn't escape unscathed. He suffered a gash on his face from flying debris.

What hurt Amerine the most wasn't his own injury. It was discovering that the three Americans who had perished were his friends: Master Sergeant Jefferson Donald "J.D." Davis, 39, of Watauga, Tennessee, a family man with two children, a sportsman who loved fishing and riding motorcycles; Sergeant First Class Daniel Petithory, 32, of Cheshire, Massachusetts, the group's cutup, a former altar boy who liked to wear Elvis-style glasses on parachute jumps; and Staff Sergeant Brian "Cody" Prosser, 28, of Bakersfield, California, known as a soldier's soldier, who had arrived on the hill the day before. Every surviving member of Amerine's team was wounded, and several, including Amerine, were eventually transported to a hospital in Germany for treatment.

A military investigation revealed that one of the men from headquarters who had arrived earlier in the day had made a horrible mistake. He was on the ground directing air strikes when he accidentally gave the wrong coordinates to a B-52 bomber that released the 2,000-pound bomb that struck the hill.

Three days later, while Amerine was recovering in Germany, the Taliban officially surrendered Kandahar, marking the end of their violent, terrorist-supporting regime. Amerine and his fellow Green Berets had done their job. They had lived up to the Special Forces' official motto, *De Oppresso Liber*, Latin for "To Liberate the Oppressed."

Two weeks after the Taliban surrendered, Hamid Karzai was named leader of the country's new transitional government. In 2004, he became the first democratically elected president of Afghanistan. He was reelected in 2009.

For their courageous stand at Tarin Kowt and their efforts to defeat the Taliban, the eleven men of ODA 574 earned three Silver Stars, five Bronze Stars with Valor, two Bronze Stars, and eleven Purple Hearts.

On January 15, 2002, Jason Amerine, who recovered from his injuries and was promoted to major, was awarded the Bronze Star with Valor and the Purple Heart. According to his citation,

"His actions in the face of overwhelming odds and direct hostile aggression resulted in the surrender of Kandahar by the Taliban forces . . . and directly contributed to his unit's and his country's success."

Lieutenant General Paul Mikolashek, who oversaw the land war in Afghanistan, praised Amerine's "exceptional courage, dedication to mission, and personal sacrifice. [His] remarkable performance and selfless commitment to his fellow comrades in arms serve as the standard for others."

Amerine, who was a guest of honor at President George W. Bush's State of the Union address in 2002, said: "Serving as an officer in the United States Army has been the greatest privilege of my life. In Afghanistan, I commanded American and Afghan soldiers, each fighting for his own nation and his people, yet united in a common cause as they entrusted one another with their lives. There is no greater courage than for people to fight side by side against the terrible odds they faced with such impenetrable faith in one another."

Air Force Staff Sergeant Alan Yoshida was awarded the Silver Star for his actions during combat on December 3 and 4, 2001.

Green Berets Master Sergeant Jefferson Donald Davis and Sergeant First Class Daniel Petithory were each posthumously awarded the Silver Star and Purple Heart. Staff Sergeant Brian Prosser was posthumously awarded the Bronze Star with Valor and the Purple Heart.

"The Americans Won't Get Out Alive"

★

LIEUTENANT STEPHEN BOADA

Marine lieutenants Stephen Boada and Sam Monte were sitting outside a mud hut with the elder of a remote village in a mountainous area known to harbor members of al-Qaeda. Nearby, 28 Marines were keeping their eyes peeled for any possible trouble.

As the two officers chatted with the local leader, their interpreter tapped Boada on the shoulder and whispered, "There's something you should know."

The interpreter pointed to his Icom radio scanner, a handheld device that picks up nearby transmissions, and said, "Radio traffic is saying, 'The Americans are here, and there are thirty of them. We're setting up an ambush. The Americans will never make it out alive.'"

It wasn't the news Boada wanted to hear, but it didn't surprise him. After all, this was known enemy territory — where no American troops had ever been before.

Boada, 27, of Bristol, Connecticut, was an artillery officer with First Battalion, Twelfth Marine Regiment. But on this deployment, he was attached to Kilo Company, Third Battalion, Third Marines, Combined Joint Task Force-76.

Hours earlier, the Marines had set out on a rainy morning in a convoy in Laghman Province. It was May 8, 2005, the third day of a week-long patrol called Operation Tar Heels. The platoon, commanded by Monte, had driven as far as it could before the road ended, so the leathernecks dismounted and walked for miles along a valley trail that led to several remote villages. The men had left behind their bulky flak vests at their patrol base and wore only their SAPI plates — two-inch-thick bulletproof plates that fit in a vest — so they would have a lighter load hiking in the mountains. Without their full body armor, they could move faster in case they came in contact with the enemy, who didn't wear any body armor.

Boada was on this patrol only because he had volunteered for it. Ever since his arrival in Afghanistan six months earlier, he had been looking for opportunities to go "outside the wire" where he felt he could do the most good. For Operation Tar Heels, he wanted to meet with tribal leaders to find out what the people needed most, such as medical supplies or veterinary visits. More important, Boada was hoping to obtain from the locals information about the brutal drug lords and al-Qaeda militants who were freely operating and living in the area.

The elders at the first two places the platoon visited were

wary and suspicious of the Americans, having never seen any until now. Boada wondered if they were acting out of fear of the drug lords, Taliban, and al-Qaeda, or out of loyalty to those groups.

It was here at the third village, Shatagal, where the Marines learned they were being targeted for an ambush. "We have to stop focusing on the villagers' basic needs and focus on our own security," Monte told Boada. The mission had changed from "meet and greet" the people to "gain and maintain" contact with the enemy. In a common military operation known as "movement to contact," the Marines went looking for the militants. Using satellite communications, the leathernecks called their base and asked their company commander for a helicopter to recon the area, but their request was denied because of bad weather. The clouds were too low.

As the Marines moved out of the village, the scanner began picking up new radio traffic from the enemy. The interpreter recognized two of the voices as al-Qaeda cell leaders who had been responsible for a rocket attack on a nearby police station a few days earlier. Then he warned the officers, "I heard them say, 'The Americans just moved past us. We'll get them on the way out.'"

Monte stopped his men and put them in a defensive formation in the valley, which was bordered by two ridges about a half mile apart separated by a river. He sent a machine-gun squad to the high ground on the west ridgeline, hoping they could spot the militants. Boada scanned the rugged slopes but couldn't see any enemy movement because of the terrain. A short while later, members of the squad reported they saw 12 men carrying automatic weapons and RPGs on the east ridgeline across from them.

As anticipated, minutes later the rest of the platoon began receiving incoming fire, so Monte ordered the machine guns to open up on the enemy. The militants scattered into a large draw — a natural depression into which water drains — and engaged in a brief firefight before disappearing into caves and rock outcroppings.

Wanting to flush them out, Boada, Monte, and the rest of the Marines in the valley trekked across the frigid river, which was chest deep in spots and rapidly flowing from snowmelt. When they reached the other side, they took positions about 200 yards away from where they suspected the enemy was hiding.

Because the clouds were parting, Boada, who was the platoon's forward observer and acting forward air controller, called in air support. Two A-10 Warthogs made four passes at the caves, firing rockets and 30-mm cannon.

With every pass, the interpreter heard on his Icom several excitable enemy transmissions such as, "They're shooting at me!" or "That rocket went just over my head!" Each transmission helped Boada get a better fix on their positions. He told the pilots, "Bring the impacts of those rounds just a little bit lower."

When the first attack jets ran out of ammo, two more Warthogs arrived and made another four passes at the caves. Then the Marines moved toward the ridgeline and swept into the draw in pairs, searching in caves and around rocks for the enemy. Boada buddied up with Sergeant Robert Campbell, one of Second Platoon's squad leaders, and peered into outcroppings and small caverns. Every time Boada poked his head in, he aimed his weapon and flashlight, ready to shoot anything that moved. He kept thinking, *I hope I see them before they see me.* Although Boada had been in the Marines for seven years and been involved in a few skirmishes, this was his first real taste of combat in Afghanistan.

Suddenly, during the cave clearing, he heard a burst of AK-47 fire about 25 yards away and then screams of "I've been hit!" and "Help me!"

One of the Marines hustled over to Boada and reported that Lance Corporal Nicholas "Nick" Kirven, who was a team leader, and Corporal Richard "Ricky" Schoener had been hit. They had been examining a dead militant when they were hit by enemy bullets spewing from a nearby cave. No one could get to the fallen Marines because they were sprawled on the ground in the kill zone, which was ablaze with enemy fire and grenades.

"We need to move closer to see where the fire is coming from and try to pull those guys to safety," said Boada.

With Campbell providing cover, Boada disregarded the bullets and leapfrogged from one rock to another to move within a few yards of the wounded men. He positioned himself behind a small rock only 13 yards away from the cave.

Monte ordered the troops to encircle the cave while Corporal Troy Arndt, a team leader, and Corporal Julian Chinana, a scout sniper, scrambled over to Boada, hoping to drag the wounded Marines to safety. Kirven wasn't moving, but Schoener was still trying to shoot, although he was severely wounded.

"We have to get our Marines, sir!" Arndt cried out to Boada. "We just have to!"

"Roger that," said Boada. "We'll throw some smoke and try to rescue them."

Chinana fired an M203 smoke grenade, but the round ricocheted off the cave's rock face and splintered. The smoke failed to mark the enemy's position or shroud the fallen men.

Losing blood from his wounds and growing weaker, Schoener attempted to point out the exact location of the enemy before he lost consciousness.

Boada then flung a smoke grenade and fired into the cave, allowing Arndt a few precious seconds to rush out and grab hold of Schoener by his SAPI vest. But just as Arndt began lugging him, the vest ripped apart and Arndt fell. By this time, the smoke was clearing, so Boada leaped out from behind his cover and, in the face of heavy machine-gun fire, he pulled Arndt behind a small rock.

Boada and Arndt were now just ten yards from the cave entrance and agonizingly close — only five feet — from their fallen comrades. Neither wounded Marine was moving. Boada didn't know if they were dead or alive, but it didn't matter. He and the rest of the leathernecks were going to do whatever it took to get those two out of the kill zone and back to their base.

"We have to find another way to pull them out of there!" Arndt shouted.

"I'll try to neutralize them with frag grenades," said Boada. He prepped a grenade to throw at the enemy position. Then, while firing his M9 pistol with his left hand, he hurled the grenade with his right hand. The deafening explosion shook the ground and showered the area with debris. He was hoping the blast would kill the militants, but they answered back by directing a volley of fire at the rock that he and Arndt had ducked behind.

Frustrated, Boada tossed another grenade, but the militants were still shooting back. "I need more grenades!" Boada hollered to Arndt.

Arndt moved toward his fellow Marines and yelled, "Who's got more grenades? Who's got more?" From as far away as 20 feet, the others tossed him their grenades with the safety lever and safety pin in place. He prepped one by taking out the thumb clip and loosening the pin. Then he tossed it ten feet to Boada, who caught it and pulled out the pin. Shouting to his men, "Covering fire!" he stood up and flung the grenade into the cave. They were laying down suppressive fire just inches over his head.

Again and again, the Marines repeated the dangerous grenade relay. Even though Boada was in the casualty radius of the blasts—the area most likely for shrapnel to kill or wound a person—he continued throwing the grenades while exposing himself to direct close-range enemy fire.

At one point during his grenade barrage, Boada was struck in the shoulder from ricocheted rounds. The impacts knocked him down, but despite the injuries and loss of blood, he continued to attack the enemy by firing his weapon and heaving a grenade at the same time.

Finally, after the fifth grenade exploded, there was no movement in the cave or any return fire.

Corporal Jason Valencia, a team leader, asked Boada, "Sir, do you want me to search the cave?"

"Absolutely."

Valencia took two Marines and carefully examined the enemy cave. He hollered to Boada, "Clear!"

While Boada helped coordinate security with Monte, Arndt and a corpsman dashed over to the two American casualties. The corpsman kneeled down next to Kirven and shook his head. "He has no pulse," he told his comrades.

Schoener was still alive, but just barely. Before he could be treated, however, his heart stopped. Frantically, the corpsman performed CPR on him. After several desperate minutes, he gave up and dropped his head. "It's no use," the corpsman said. "He's gone."

Seeing the anguished looks of the Marines closest to the bodies, Boada told them, "Let's all get back behind cover. We've lost two. I don't want to lose any more." *We can't afford to get too emotional*, he thought. *I have to bring the rest back alive. That's priority one.* He knew the leathernecks were hurting emotionally. He was, too. He had been on an earlier 45-day mission with this same band of brothers and got to know each of them, including Schoener and Kirven.

The two young infantry riflemen had come from different backgrounds and had opposite personalities, but they had formed a strong bond in Afghanistan and had become best friends.

Schoener, 22, from tiny Hayes, Louisiana, graduated with honors from Bell City High School, where he was prom king and senior class president. He had plans to attend college, but the 9/11 terrorist attacks prompted the bright, quiet student to postpone school and join the Marines. He told his family that if anybody had to take a bullet to save a buddy, he wanted to be the one.

Kirven, 21, of Richmond, Virginia, was the jokester of the platoon, pulling pranks and always finding the humor in the most serious situations. Squad members liked to tease him and call him "Paris" (after socialite Paris Hilton) because of his flashy style of dress and of the care he took fixing his hair when he was off duty. He had joined the Marines at age 17 because he felt he needed more structure in his life. He was only three weeks away from ending his tour of duty when he was killed.

Now two Marines would be heading home in flag-draped coffins.

Boada called back to the base for a helicopter to transport the bodies, but he was told the clouds were too low for the chopper to get in. That meant the leathernecks would have to carry their dead comrades six miles over rugged terrain in enemy-infested territory throughout the night.

The Marines wrapped the bodies in ponchos and at 6 P.M. began the dreadful duty of taking turns carrying their lifeless comrades down the mountain toward the patrol base.

There wasn't much talking. They concentrated on the task at hand, which was to make sure no one else was killed as they slowly worked their way back.

About a half hour after they started down, the interpreter told Boada that he heard some disturbing chatter on the scanner. "They said, 'The Americans won't get out alive. We're going to get them. We have about thirty people heading north to ambush them.'"

Boada radioed for help. Soon one heavily armed AC-130 gunship flew overhead. Because the sun was setting, the crew used equipment that allowed them to see in the dark. The pilot, whose call sign was Sniper 2-1, confirmed through infrared devices the Marines' location and then searched for the militants who were setting up the ambush.

Within minutes, Sniper 2-1 radioed Boada, "We've got fourteen individuals moving north toward your position. It looks like they're armed. Do we have permission to engage?"

It's pretty obvious who those guys are and what they're up to, Boada thought. He gave the crew clearance to shoot at the enemy. "You're cleared hot," he radioed. Within seconds, the plane's 105-mm cannon echoed throughout the valley. Then everything turned quiet.

Less than a minute later, the pilot reported to Boada, "This is Sniper Two-One. Fourteen targets have been neutralized."

A smile crept across Boada's face, knowing the militants were dead. "Roger that."

Later, the pilot radioed him that another 15 enemy fighters were in front of the leathernecks in an obvious ambush-ready position. The plane came in low to attack them. Knowing what had happened to their companions, the militants dashed into a building in a small village that was several hundred yards from the Marines.

Sniper 2-1 kept Boada informed with constant updates: "No movement . . . no movement . . . okay . . . contact. I've got movement. They're heading north again toward your position."

Once more, Boada gave the pilot clearance to attack. The plane roared in and let loose with its armament. The militants fled in all directions, but they couldn't escape the gunship's firepower. When the shooting stopped, Sniper 2-1 radioed Boada, "All fifteen targets neutralized."

After those two attacks, the plane remained in the sky looking out for the Marines' welfare throughout their difficult nighttime hike. *What a blessing that gunship is*, Boada thought.

Shortly before sunrise, the emotionally drained and tired leathernecks reached their vehicles. What started out as a planned six-hour patrol ended after a 22-hour ordeal. They sat down, guzzled water, and took stock of what they had just endured. One of the first things Boada did was pull out a picture of his wife, Jenny, that he always kept in the pocket of his cargo pants. He stared at her smiling face for a long time until he was interrupted by Chinana.

Flashing a grin, the corporal said, "Look what I just pulled out of my forehead." He opened his palm and showed a piece of shrapnel that had struck him the previous day.

"What more proof do we need that you're a hardhead," Boada joked.

The little bit of levity vanished when he caught a glimpse of the two wrapped bodies in the back of a Humvee. Next to them stood their closest pals in mourning.

They are coping really well over our loss, Boada told himself. *We got through the night safely because they understood our goal was to get back in one piece. They did a great job. I couldn't ask for a better platoon of Marines.*

On February 1, 2006, Stephen Boada was awarded the Silver Star for "his bold leadership, wise judgment, and complete dedication to duty" on that fateful day, according to his citation. It added that his ability to direct the Warthogs' strikes against the ambush-ready enemy during the platoon's nighttime march "saved many lives."

After the ceremony, Boada told reporters, "The Marines I was with that day deserve the recognition. They all need to be talked about more than me. They are all amazing."

Added Boada, who received a Purple Heart for his injuries and was promoted to captain, "I think about what happened out there every day and will for as long as I live. I think about what we could have done differently, what we could have done to have those two Marines walk home with us."

Corporal Troy Arndt, 22, earned a Bronze Star with Valor for his brave actions on that day.

Lance Corporal Nicholas "Nick" Kirven and Corporal Richard "Ricky" Schoener were both posthumously awarded a Bronze Star and Purple Heart for their part in the cave-clearing incident. Said Lieutenant Sam Monte at the memorial service for the two fallen Marines, "They didn't give up, and they didn't let any of us give up."

The Fatal Funnel

MASTER SERGEANT SARUN SAR

Master Sergeant Sarun Sar's boots crunched in the snow as he crept up to the windowless stone-and-earth mountain hut. Inside lurked the Taliban fighter whom Sar had been chasing.

Is he the only one inside or are there more? wondered Sar, leader of a 12-man Special Forces team that had helicoptered onto a high ridge where Taliban were hiding. He glanced over his shoulder, expecting to see some of his fellow Green Berets right behind him. But he was surprised to discover he was alone. The rest of his men were still pinned down several hundred yards away by heavy enemy fire.

Pursuing a Taliban fighter in knee-deep snow in the thin high-altitude air while wearing 50 pounds of gear had left the compact five-foot four-inch, 120-pound soldier breathing hard. Nevertheless, he was still poised to strike. Sar might have been

America's smallest Special Forces warrior, but pound for pound he was one of the toughest — and one of the most fearless. Like every Green Beret, he possessed uncommon grit and guts. But unlike his comrades, Sar was molded by a childhood of anguish and suffering in a land of death known as "the killing fields."

I have to go in there, thought Sar, his M4 assault rifle trained on the partially opened door of the hut. *But I better wait for backup.* After the team's medic joined him, Sar peered into the opening and saw only blackness inside. "I'll go first," he whispered.

Flicking on the flashlight mounted on the barrel of his M4, Sar bolted into the small, low doorway and pointed the weapon straight ahead. But his bulky patrol gear snagged on the sides of the narrow entrance.

Sar was stuck halfway in the murky hut for only a second or two. It was enough time for him to see the illuminated face of the Taliban fighter he had been chasing. And it was enough time to see the muzzle of the man's AK-47 pointed directly at his head from just six feet away.

It was not, however, enough time for Sar to duck. The militant fired a short burst, *bang . . . bang . . . bang!* Sar felt the heat from the muzzle blasts as they lit up the smoky darkness. Miraculously, two of the bullets missed him, but one struck the lower left edge of his Kevlar helmet by his forehead. The jarring impact felt like a hammer blow to his skull. "I'm hit! I'm hit!" he screamed, falling back out of the doorway.

They say that when you face death, your life flashes before you. For Sarun Sar, it was a life that was nearly way too brief.

As a boy in the late 1960s and early 1970s, Sarun led a carefree childhood on the family rice farm in the Southeast Asian country of Cambodia. His father was a respected schoolteacher in the town of Phnom Srong, and his mother took care of the home. When they weren't in class, Sarun and his two sisters and three brothers tended to the chickens, cows, and pigs as well as the rice paddies. His loving parents made a comfortable home for the kids and encouraged them to read, learn, and think for themselves.

In 1975, when Sarun was in the fourth grade, war devastated his country and his boyhood. Communist insurgents known as the Khmer Rouge overthrew the Cambodian government, triggering a national nightmare. Led by ruthless dictator Pol Pot, the Khmer Rouge evicted hundreds of thousands of men, women, and children from their homes in cities and towns and shipped them to the countryside for forced labor.

An untold number of families, including Sarun's, were split up. His father was arrested and sent to a prison camp. His mother and siblings were hauled away. Sarun was taken to a commune where, as part of a child-labor force, he dug irrigation canals, ponds, and dams, tended to cattle, and worked in the rice fields. When the rainy season started, he and the other children awakened at 4 A.M. to plant rice, toiled all day, and returned to their commune at 7 P.M. to eat a skimpy meal that had little nutritional value. Then they attended "livelihood meetings," which were nothing more than brainwashing sessions, between 9 and 11 P.M. They were told that family relationships were banned because, as the Khmer Rouge falsely claimed, parents mentally abused their children and took advantage of them — which was exactly what the Khmer Rouge were doing to those same children.

In their efforts to "reeducate" the children, the Khmer Rouge praised communism and lied to them about "evil" Americans and "wicked" democracy. But Sarun refused to believe any of it, because he had been an avid reader and had learned from his father. The boy knew the truth. He boldly spoke up at these brainwashing sessions, but was punished for his beliefs by being deprived of food or being forced to work longer hours. He soon learned to keep his mouth shut. But that didn't mean he believed the propaganda. Most of the children accepted whatever they were taught, because they had no other way to learn the truth. Books and radios were banned in the communes.

Not having seen or heard from his parents or any of his siblings for four years, Sarun assumed he was an orphan. He had good reason to think he was the family's lone survivor.

Adults worked in the rice fields for 12 hours a day without adequate rest or food. Many, especially those who were raised in the city and weren't used to manual labor, became ill and died in the paddies. Those who did not meet their quota were marched to distant fields where they were forced to dig their own graves before Khmer Rouge soldiers slaughtered them. These death sites became forever known as "the killing fields."

To the merciless Khmer Rouge, the lives of the workers had little or no value, so even a minor infraction was enough reason to send them to the killing fields. For example, if you were caught eating grass or even insects to ease your hunger, you were executed. Contacting a relative without permission could get you killed. So could practicing Buddhism, the religion in which Sarun had been raised. Families of previous Cambodian soldiers and government workers — including teachers — were often forced to work themselves to death. Those who managed to survive for a year or two were eventually charged with being enemies of the state and slain.

The boy witnessed countless murders, especially of the educated. The Khmer Rouge believed that the persons who presented the greatest danger to the regime were knowledgeable, well-read, and intelligent. Illiterate peasants, on the other hand, were willing to accept the lies that the Khmer Rouge fed them.

So the soldiers systematically tried to kill those who were deemed "educated." If you spoke a foreign language, you would die. If you wore glasses, you would die. If you owned a book, you would die. Anyone who was educated or was a business owner had to fake being ignorant and poor in order to survive. During Sarun's childhood, 1.7 million Cambodians died from starvation or were executed in the killing fields.

Such torment in the early years of life can either weaken or strengthen a child's heart and will. For Sarun, it strengthened them.

In 1978, when Sarun was 12, he and the other boys were given military training while working on the communal farm. They were taught how to shoot rifles and how to maneuver during jungle warfare. Because there was no way to receive news, Sarun didn't know that Cambodia's neighbor, Vietnam, had invaded the country in a bloody attempt to overthrow the Khmer Rouge. So Sarun and the other boys were surprised when they were unexpectedly given uniforms and told they must help defend their country.

They were now members of a corps of Cambodian child soldiers who were taught to "follow orders without hesitation."

In his first taste of combat, Sarun did what he was trained to do—shoot at the enemy. He found combat exciting and thrilling. But that impression quickly changed to shock when half his squad—made up of teenage boys—was either killed or wounded.

Even though he was the youngest in his unit, Sarun grew braver with every new firefight. He discovered something about himself: He was a natural-born soldier and a sharpshooting rifleman who relished the chance to inflict damage on the enemy. Never mind that he was fighting for a beastly government that had wiped out his family. His country—which he had been taught to love by his father before the Khmer Rouge took power—was being invaded, and he felt it was his duty to defend it.

Sarun had been slightly wounded several times in combat, but had avoided any serious injuries during the first months of the war. One morning while he was on patrol with his squad, the young soldiers were walking single file on a jungle path when the boy in front of Sarun tripped a land mine. It exploded, killing the boy and badly hurting Sarun, who suffered shrapnel wounds to his hands and feet.

Sarun was taken to the Kao-I-Dang refugee camp operated by the United Nations along the border of Thailand and Cambodia. There, he spent several weeks recovering from his injuries. During that time, the Vietnamese army defeated the Khmer Rouge.

While in the camp, Sarun was stunned to learn that his older sister was alive in a village in Cambodia. He left the camp and made the dangerous journey to find her. After a joyous and tearful reunion, he led her back to Kao-I-Dang.

Soon his worst fears were realized: He was told that his mother and missing siblings had died of starvation and that his older brother was executed after being caught smuggling weapons for anti-Vietnamese guerrillas. Sarun later learned that his father had survived the Khmer Rouge's reign of terror, but was imprisoned by the Vietnamese for treason and died behind bars from illness.

In 1980, Sarun and his sister were given the biggest break of their lives. Under the sponsorship of a Presbyterian church in Rockville, Maryland, they immigrated to the United States. He arrived on American soil with four dollars in his pocket, no English, and no idea of his real birth date. Immigration officials gave him a new birthday—May 15, 1966.

Under the foster care of a family from the church's congregation, Sarun attended high school. Although it was a challenge for a boy from the jungles of war-torn Cambodia to fit into the comfy lifestyle of suburbia, he slowly made the adjustment. He competed on the wrestling, cross-country, and track teams, and he earned spending money sweeping floors in a print shop and washing dishes in a restaurant. His sister, meanwhile, moved to California.

When Sarun graduated in 1985, he joined the U.S. Army because, as he told his friends, "I want to serve my adopted country." The following year, Sarun Sar was sworn in as a U.S. citizen. Choosing to make the military his career, he decided that if he was going to be a full-time soldier, he wanted to be a member of the Army Special Forces. More than 80 percent of those who try to qualify for this elite unit fail to meet the physically and mentally demanding requirements. Over and over, Sar heard that he was too small to make the grade. But that scorn only pushed him on to greater effort, because he was determined to prove the naysayers wrong. And he succeeded.

Sar fought in the first Persian Gulf War in 1990 and was later deployed to 15 countries such as Thailand, Cambodia, Bosnia, Kosovo, and Colombia. Between his deployments, he earned a bachelor's degree in American history at Campbell University in North Carolina and a master's degree in leadership and management at Webster University in St. Louis.

As a member of Seventh Special Forces Group, Sar saw action in Afghanistan in 2003 and again in 2005. When he arrived in country for the second time, he and his team were engaged in as many as six or seven attacks a day.

Eventually, he was able to focus on his primary goal: gaining the trust of the tribal mountain people in Paktika Province, one of the poorest areas in Afghanistan. They were vulnerable, they were afraid, and they wanted someone to protect them against the Taliban. It was a difficult task at first.

If the enemy thought a village was cooperating with Sar, they shelled it at night with 107-mm rockets and mortars and hid IEDs in the roads to spread fear. When Sar's team helped build a small town hall and a school, the Taliban blew up the hall and tried to burn down the school.

But Sar and his men persevered and routed Taliban fighters time and again. The Americans soon were providing security and health care and constructing classrooms, clinics, and town halls. They helped establish an infrastructure for water, sewer, and electricity. On their days off, they taught English to children, played soccer with them, and handed out clothes donated from home.

Sar attended weekly *shuras*, meetings held with tribal elders to allow them to voice their concerns. At first the village leaders were surprised to see someone like him, because he didn't fit the image of the American soldier. He was short and Cambodian-born. But having grown up in a country of horror, Sar possessed a profound understanding of the oppressed Afghans.

Within four months of their arrival in the region, Sar and his team had won the trust of the villagers, who, in turn, provided him with valuable intelligence concerning the Taliban. About once or twice a week, Sar and his men engaged in small skirmishes with the enemy—but nothing like what happened on March 5, 2005.

On that cold, foggy morning, Sar, who was the team sergeant of Operational Detachment Alpha 732, set out with his 12-man A-team on an armed reconnaissance of a suspected Taliban hideout in a mountaintop village 9,000 feet above sea level. Two UH-60 Blackhawk helicopters—each carrying six members of the team—skimmed over rugged, snowy peaks. The men were scanning the area for signs of Taliban activity when Sar ordered the choppers to land on opposite sides of a ridge near several suspicious earth and stone huts.

From his helicopter, Sar watched the first Blackhawk touch down on the north side of the ridge less than 100 yards below the huts. Six men jumped out of the chopper and immediately came under intense automatic-weapons fire from the village and nearby woods. Returning fire, the soldiers sought cover behind snow-swept rocks and trees.

Sar's copter was starting its descent on the south side of the ridge. Seeing the Taliban shooting at his men, Sar didn't wait for the Blackhawk to land. He leaped out while it was still six feet in the air.

"Follow me!" he shouted. The others hit the ground running.

As a veteran of numerous combat operations over the previous 15 years, Sar knew his small force needed to quickly suppress the enemy fire coming from the high ground. If the Taliban kept that advantageous position, his team could be wiped out, and the Blackhawks could be damaged or destroyed if they tried to land again and rescue them.

Braving a hail of bullets, Sar charged toward the huts. Despite the heavy pack he carried, he bounded uphill, lifting his knees high in the deep snow. He had his M4 carbine set on semi-automatic, choosing his single shots carefully because there were innocent villagers in the area. He didn't want to accidentally hurt any of the locals whose confidence and trust he and his men had been working so long and hard to earn.

Sar pushed ahead and soon turned around to yell out instructions to his team. That was when he realized he was out front, alone. The rest of his men were either pinned down or laying suppressive fire.

The Taliban who had fired down at the Americans on the north side of the ridge turned their attention to the short, wiry soldier hopping in the snow toward them. Now Sar had the enemy shooting at him from one direction while his team was shooting over his head from the opposite direction. It didn't matter to him. He continued firing his weapon in his assault toward the huts. Along the way, his well-aimed shots made several militants retreat.

But three Taliban fighters figured they could overpower one lone man and rushed toward Sar. He killed the first attacker, prompting the other two to turn and run off. Sar chased after them. As he closed in on them, one of the militants dropped his weapon and screamed at Sar before taking off again. *He's no longer a threat to me*, Sar thought. *I can't shoot him in the back. I have to let him go.*

But the other militant squeezed off a few more rounds at Sar and then made a beeline for one of the huts. Sar wasn't going to let him escape. During the pursuit, Sar yelled into his radio headset at his comrades, "I'm heading for the huts. Catch up to me as fast as you can!"

The militant dashed into a hut and closed the door partway. Sar arrived moments later, but chose not to make a move until at least one other teammate showed up. Although he was itching to burst into the hut and take out the enemy, he needed a moment to catch his breath.

While he waited, a bullet grazed his leg. Once again, he shouted into his headset, "Someone get over here now!"

The first person to reach him was the team's medic. "I'll go first," Sar whispered. He rushed into the doorway and got stuck in what's known in close combat as the "fatal funnel." It's the dangerous area where the assaulter is silhouetted against a light background from outside, making him an easy target to see from inside. Before Sar could move, the militant fired three shots from point-blank range.

One of the bullets creased the left side of Sar's Kevlar helmet, snapping his head back and slicing through the upper part of his chin strap. "I'm hit! I'm hit!" Sar screamed, his head pounding as if it had been struck by a hammer. He staggered out of the doorway, disoriented and dazed.

The medic took off Sar's helmet and searched for a bullet wound. After a quick examination, the medic gave a whistle of amazement and said, "Man, are you lucky. The round just grazed you. You're not bleeding. You have a scratch and a bump on your forehead, but otherwise you're good."

I'm good! Sar told himself. *It's not my turn to die. If I'm supposed to die, I'll die. But if three bullets that close can't kill me, then I know I'm coming home no matter what.*

Ignoring the headache and clearing his mind from his brush with death, Sar whipped out a grenade and tossed it inside. Seconds after the blast, he reentered the hut. The militant was dead. But the opposite end of the shelter presented a sight that made him cringe. Two villagers had suffered shrapnel wounds to their arms and legs.

One of the victims was a teenage boy. For a brief uncomfortable moment, Sar was transported back to the jungles of Cambodia, back to when he was a boy soldier, back to when he had suffered shrapnel wounds to his arms and legs.

Shaking that childhood image from his mind, Sar bent down and told the teenage Afghan, "You'll be all right. We'll fix you up." Sar turned to the medic and said, "Take care of them."

Sar joined the rest of the team, which had now reached the huts, and together pressed the fight until the Taliban fighters were defeated. Fortunately, none of the Green Berets was injured.

When reinforcements arrived, Sar and his men cleared each structure, room by room. Then they launched a thorough search for a suspected weapons cache. During their sweep of the village, they uncovered a large collection of RPGs, grenade launchers, a radio, a mortar and shells, bomb-making materials and explosives, and a slew of AK-47 assault rifles.

After the battle, Sar checked in on the two injured Afghan civilians. Although their wounds weren't life threatening, he arranged for them to be evacuated to a military hospital.

A few months later, Sar had completed his deployment. As the plucky Green Beret made the rounds of several villages to say good-bye, one of the tribal leaders gave him the best compliment: "I never met someone so small who was as big a warrior as you."

Promoted to sergeant major, Sarun Sar received the Silver Star for the bravery he showed during the battle of March 5, 2005.

Brigadier General David P. Fridovich, Commander, Special Operations Command, Pacific, said the medal was awarded to recognize Sar's achievements and "what he has given back to the nation." During the ceremony, Fridovich told Sar, "You've already given us so much more in return than we could ever repay you."

Humbled by the honor, Sar said that what he had done on that day was "just my duty as a soldier, protecting my guys like they protect me."

For separate actions during another firefight in Afghanistan, Sar was awarded the Bronze Star with Valor.

"Coming from Cambodia, I know what it's like to lose freedom and to suffer the loss of family," said Sar, adding, he joined the military to protect freedom and lives. He said that whatever danger he faces as a soldier is "a small price to pay for living in a country that I love more than my birthplace."

The Battle of Ebrahimkhel

STAFF SERGEANT JASON "JAKE" KIMBERLING

Staff Sergeant Jason "Jake" Kimberling and two fellow members of an air force security team examined the smoldering Afghan police checkpoint that had just been battered by RPGs and mortar rounds from a Taliban hit-and-run attack.

"We want to chase them down," a furious Afghan officer declared. "Attacks have been going on most every night. We're losing officers at the rate of three a week and morale is low. If we don't go after the Taliban now, the attacks will just keep happening. They're not going to stop, so we must kill or capture the enemy now."

Kimberling understood the officer's frustration and anger. Intelligence reports revealed that several new Taliban commanders had moved into the area and stepped up their violence against police, local leaders, villagers, and even kids. One Taliban chief was such a fanatic that he beat up schoolchildren and burned their hands with a hot iron because they had touched a book other than the Koran, Islam's holiest book. He also killed two teachers in cold blood solely because they were doing their jobs.

Reports like these infuriated Kimberling, 36, a 15-year air force veteran. As a member of 755th Expeditionary Mission Support Group, Provincial Reconstruction Team, he had been in country for eight months training the local police. He had seen plenty of Taliban-triggered bloodshed and carnage.

One of the enemy's favorite targets was where he was standing now — at a police checkpoint about 15 miles from his base in Qalat Province. On this sweltering 115-degree morning, August 8, 2006, Kimberling, Senior Airman Phillip King, and Tech Sergeant Mark Wenell had rushed to the scene in a six-vehicle convoy loaded with 15 ANP officers and 20 ANA soldiers. The three Americans were a little bleary-eyed after being up most of the previous night defending their base against a nasty rocket-and-mortar raid. But they were primed now as they headed off with their Afghan comrades in pursuit of the dozen Taliban insurgents who attacked the checkpoint. The convoy was supposed to be joined by a group of Romanian soldiers who had the communications equipment and a powerful machine gun. But because of a misunderstanding, the Romanians had returned to their base.

Kimberling was concerned about the lack of communications. All he had was a cell phone with no signal, while his interpreter, an Afghan college student nicknamed Hank, held an Icom portable radio scanner. From the backseat of a Humvee, the two kept a lookout for any trouble. Up front were King, who was driving, and Wenell, the team leader. In the truck's open bed sat an Afghan soldier armed with RPGs. No one knew his name, so they referred to him as "RPG Guy."

Their vehicle was in the middle of the convoy as it roared down Route 1, the country's major paved highway, in pursuit of the fleeing attackers. The trucks soon went off road, splashed through a shallow river, and then sped along a dusty, single-lane, rocky road that ran up into a draw where five small villages formed a semicircle.

Hearing the mounting chatter over the Icom, Hank told the three airmen, "The Taliban know we're here. They're shouting, 'The army is coming with the police.' They're telling the villagers, 'You need to run off.'"

"It's a little bit unnerving when you actually hear the enemy talking about you," Kimberling said. "It's likely they're setting us up for an ambush. They'll probably let us come all the way in and then try to close the door behind us [as a trap]. We need to prepare for the worst and hope for the best."

Like the rest of the troops, Kimberling was getting increasingly nervous. But there was no turning back.

When the convoy reached the draw, he was struck with how peaceful and lush the area looked. The tiny villages ringing the draw seemed prosperous and were surrounded by staggered rice and wheat fields, groves of almond trees, and grassland where goats were grazing.

As the unit neared the first village, a tribesman fired a few potshots at the lead truck, but was quickly captured by the ANP. He was part of a common enemy ploy: The Taliban fighters hand a villager a weapon and order him, "When the soldiers come, shoot at them. If you don't, we'll come back and kill you." Usually in that situation, the villager steps out into plain view of the troops and fires the weapon in the air or deliberately misses. Then he drops the gun and puts his hands up. That way, he's less likely to be killed. The coalition soldiers will spare him because he surrendered, and the Taliban will do likewise because he met their demand of slowing down the troops.

Kimberling, King, and Wenell joined ANA soldiers in a search of the village, looking for any weapons caches or signs of the enemy. They also spoke to an elder who said that the Taliban had just passed through. The ANP drove up to the next village, Shuhay, which was located on a plateau, and began chasing the Taliban vehicles out into the open desert toward the Pakistan border.

When the Icom traffic began to increase, the interpreter gulped. "There are many, many more than twelve Taliban fighters in this area," Hank told Kimberling. "Several enemy units say they're watching us move." What made it more disturbing was hearing some of them speaking in the native languages of Pakistan, Saudi Arabia, and Chechnya.

"That probably means al-Qaeda is here with the Taliban," said Kimberling. "That's sure to make life harder for us. The Taliban typically hit and run. But when they're with al-Qaeda, they have a tendency to fight to the last man."

Hank told Kimberling, "I'm getting more traffic. Someone asked, 'Are we going to attack them?' The answer was, 'Yes. They're a small force, and we're much larger.'"

The three Americans and the ANA soldiers moved up to the plateau so they would be in a better defensive position in case of an attack. While they waited for the ANP to return, King tried to make contact with the base defense-operations center in Qalat to give them an update and call for backup. But he was using a bulky, unreliable 35-year-old ANA radio, so he wasn't sure if his message had gotten through.

King then walked over to Kimberling and, pointing to the fields and nearby compounds, asked, "Notice anything?"

After a quick glance, Kimberling replied, "Yeah, the farmers are leaving their fields, and the women are hustling their children into their homes. It's turning into a ghost town. My gut tells me we're about to get into a knock-down, drag-out fight."

When the ANP returned an hour later without having captured any insurgents, Kimberling was leaning over the hood of his Humvee, studying maps of the area.

"What's our situation, Jake?" Wenell asked.

"The Romanians didn't show up, so we have no heavy weapons. No one knows exactly where we are, due to bad or no communications, which means no support. There are a big-time number of bad guys in the villages below us, and they know we're here. It's twelve miles back to Route 1, and it will be dark in four hours. Basically, Mark, we're on our own, and there's a seventy percent chance we're going to get hit.

"I suggest that the convoy head back through the villages with the goal of making it as close to the highway as possible so we can pick up a communications signal and call for backup, and hopefully keep everyone in one piece."

The convoy — with the Americans' truck lined up third — headed toward the lower village of Ebrahimkhel. As the road swept down toward the river, the vehicles entered an S-curve where walled-in compounds stood on both sides. When the convoy came through the turn, Kimberling asked King to slow down and put more space between their Humvee and the second truck. "If the guys in front get blown up by an RPG, I don't want to be part of them," Kimberling said.

Just as King let up on the accelerator, a wall off their right side five yards away exploded in a shower of dust and debris. "RPG!" Wenell yelled. Pointing to a small three-sided courtyard, he ordered King, "Hard right and pull into that cul-de-sac!"

A flurry of enemy RPG rounds fired from a compound 300 yards away was accompanied by a barrage of machine-gun and small-arms fire from a house 50 yards away. The enemy also shot from a nearby almond grove as well as two other positions.

Kimberling, who had a fear of dying inside a truck, was ready to leap out. "I'm not dying in here," he declared.

King maneuvered the Humvee into the cul-de-sac so that it provided cover for the rest of the troops. The vehicle hadn't even stopped when Kimberling jumped out and began firing back. "Keep the truck running!" he shouted to King. Earlier in the day, King had turned off the engine, and it had locked up because of the oppressive heat. "Whatever you do, don't turn off the truck!"

Kimberling dashed into the danger zone and began shooting his way to a wall that looked down on the main enemy positions. King was right on his heels, entering the fray by firing his M4 carbine, while Wenell let loose with his M203 grenade launcher. Even though Kimberling had experienced combat before in Afghanistan and Iraq, he had never seen such massive fire coming from so many different directions. An RPG was exploding near his comrades and him about every five seconds during the first two minutes.

One of the rockets blasted into the wall that he and King were using for cover. The shock wave from the explosion threw the two men back about eight feet, and both landed hard on the ground. Kimberling felt as if he had been hit by a truck. He was dizzy and had an awful sensation that his insides, especially his brains, were scrambled.

He rolled over and stared at King, who was struggling to get his bearings, and said, "Phil, I hear bells ringing."

King was too dazed to speak at first. His head throbbed, and his hearing was bad. He would later learn he'd suffered a concussion.

"Are you good, Phil?" Kimberling asked. "Are you good?" When King nodded slowly, Kimberling helped him to his feet and said, "Let's get back to the wall."

Only the top part of the wall had been sheered off by the blast, so it still provided cover as they fired back. Whatever fear they felt — the racing heart, the sweaty palms, the dry mouth — during the first enemy volley had vanished. Their battle instincts and training had kicked in, and they were now in combat mode. So was Wenell, who was standing on top of one of the Humvees' tires for a better shooting angle.

When Kimberling peered over the wall, he saw a Taliban assault force running up the hill toward the cul-de-sac. The leader of that group was firing his automatic weapon from his hip on a dead run. While bullets were slamming into the wall, Kimberling was vigorously returning fire. His perfectly placed shots to the chest killed two, including the assault leader. Kimberling's actions gave his fellow troops time to regroup and eliminate additional insurgents, temporarily halting the charge.

Concentrated machine-gun fire soon was flying from five different positions as bullets ricocheted off walls and trucks. Despite a pounding headache, King exposed himself to enemy fire while he directed the Afghan soldiers and policemen to move to better shooting positions. The troops were following the Americans' lead, doing everything that was asked of them.

Controlling the high ground on a steep hill gave the troops an important advantage. But in this battle, the enemy also had an advantage — two to three times more men.

After another enemy charge, several insurgents made it all the way to the base of the protective wall. Kimberling was slipping a new magazine into his weapon when a militant's rifle appeared over the wall, aimed at King, who was too busy firing his weapon to see it. Kimberling kicked King in the rear and out of the line of fire just as the insurgent shot between them.

An Afghan soldier next to them grabbed the barrel of the rifle and yanked it out of the militant's hand. Seconds later, an enemy hand grenade flew over the wall. But another Afghan — at four feet nine inches, the shortest member among the troops — used his hand like a tennis racquet and slapped the grenade while it was still in the air. The grenade sailed back over to the Taliban's side of the wall and exploded.

The Afghan troops began laughing. "This is great!" one of them yelled to Kimberling. "We are killing many Taliban!"

"I'm glad you're happy," the American replied.

A moment later, after spotting an insurgent breaking through an opening in the wall, Kimberling dropped him with a few well-aimed bullets. An Afghan soldier then snatched all the ammo off the body.

Turning to King, Kimberling said, "Phil, throughout my life, all I wanted to be was a fishing guide. A day like this sure reinforces that dream."

King couldn't help it. In the heat of life-and-death combat, he burst out laughing.

Kimberling looked over the wall and saw that several militants had made it from the almond grove to a spot below the cul-de-sac, so he raked them with his M4. The Taliban fighters responded by pummeling the wall with a torrent of machine-gun fire and more RPGs from their fortified compound.

The troops aimed their own RPGs at the compound, but their rockets weren't penetrating its thick wall. Some actually bounced off.

Wenell dashed back to the truck and pulled out an old M72 light antitank weapon (LAW) that was manufactured in the late 1960s for use in the Vietnam War. He had obtained the bazooka-like weapon from a forgotten crate that had been stuffed in the rear of one of the base camps. No one was sure it would work. But he brought it with him because it was much lighter than its more modern cousin, the AT4. Kimberling and King always made fun of Wenell's LAW and even stuck My Little Pony stickers on it.

"Hey, put some heat on that house," Wenell ordered the troops. When they laid down a heavy burst of firepower, he scampered out beyond the wall and kneeled in a shooting position in a shallow ditch.

"This could go either way," Kimberling told King. "It's either going to knock down the wall of the compound, or it's going to blow up right here, and his head is going to fall off."

Without any hesitation, Wenell fired the LAW. Despite its age, the old rocket flew straight and true and slammed into the compound's wall, blowing open a large hole. The Afghan soldiers cheered and fired three RPGs right into the same gap. Seconds later, a deafening explosion shook the ground and sent a fiery cloud 300 feet in the air. "Wow," marveled Kimberling. "I guess we found their weapons cache."

"That put them on their heels!" King gloated.

"This is our chance, Phil," said Kimberling. "Get the truck."

King scampered into the truck while Kimberling ran over to Wenell and said, "Hey, we gotta go!" He grabbed Wenell's body armor to help him to his feet when an insurgent rounded the corner just four feet away. Both Americans shot him twice in the chest, but he didn't drop. He just stood there, swaying. "Our rounds passed right through him," said Kimberling. "He doesn't know he's dead yet." Lowering a shoulder, Kimberling slammed into him and watched him topple to the ground.

Before they could rush to the Humvee, Wenell said, "I forgot to crush the tube." With Kimberling providing cover, Wenell stomped on the LAW until it broke. He wanted to make sure the Taliban wouldn't be able to use it to make an IED.

As the two ran toward their vehicle, they were strafed by a militant standing on the roof about 20 feet away. The bullets hissed and zipped past their heads, between their legs, and at their feet before the insurgent ducked behind a wall.

The two airmen froze and stared at each other in disbelief. "Holy smokes," whistled Kimberling. "We should be goners."

"He had us dead to rights."

"Uh, maybe we should shoot back."

They both started firing at the militant's rooftop position until Kimberling yelled to Wenell, "Go, go, go! I've got this." Kimberling stood out in the open, giving cover to Wenell and other troops who were scurrying to their vehicles. With nowhere to hide, Kimberling zigzagged toward the house, making himself a difficult target. But now bullets were whipping by his head from other Taliban fighters who had reached the wall that Kimberling had used for cover.

Just then an Afghan soldier darted over to Kimberling, snatched a grenade off the American's web gear, and hurled it onto the roof. The explosion sent up a ball of red mist, prompting Kimberling to say, "He's gone. Okay. He's gone."

"Two for one," the Afghan rejoiced.

Kimberling knew what he meant. Although he saw only one person on the roof, he had seen, at the beginning of the fight, the same insurgent on top of the house with a boy—possibly his son—by his side.

Before all the troops could reach their vehicles, the militants had charged up the hill and over the wall, so Kimberling and seven soldiers lay on the ground, spreading enough firepower to slow down the assault.

"Pull back! We're moving out!" King shouted.

Kimberling dove into the Humvee as it squealed out of the cul-de-sac. The truck, which was in the middle of the convoy, started down the hill with RPG Guy launching rockets out the back. Enemy gunners from different parts of the village continued to hound the troops.

As the vehicle was taking sniper fire from rooftops and small-arms fire from the almond grove, Wenell and Kimberling looked out the windows for enemy RPGs. Seeing one zooming toward them from the right, Wenell yelled to King, "Brakes!" King hit the brakes as the deadly rocket skimmed inches across the hood of their Humvee. Spotting another enemy RPG zeroing in on them from the left side, Kimberling hollered, "Gas! Gas! Gas!" That rocket whizzed a few feet past the truck's backside.

"Nothing like playing Frogger with your life," said Kimberling, referring to the old video game.

Suddenly, the vehicle in front of them swerved toward a steep embankment because an IED had exploded, taking out a large chunk of road and damaging the lead truck. After veering off to the right, the other vehicles moved sideways at a sharp 45-degree angle along the embankment. The airmen's Humvee was almost on its side, forcing Kimberling to plant his foot on the doorjamb to keep from falling against the left rear passenger door. At the same time, he had a tight grip on King's flak vest to keep him off the driver's side front door.

Despite the dicey situation, Kimberling cracked, "This is great. We're getting shot at from all sides. We're in a soft-top Humvee about ready to tip over. And somehow RPG Guy is hanging on in the back. This is like a circus act!"

The embankment soon leveled out so that none of the vehicles was in danger of flipping. But then the truck in front of the Americans got stuck. King hollered, "I'll take care of this!" He gunned the engine and rammed his Humvee into the back of the Afghans' truck, knocking it free and pushing it toward a knoll, where the rest of the troops were gathering by a tiny, abandoned 12-foot-by-12-foot mud-walled shack.

When they reached the knoll, Kimberling jumped out and hustled over to an Afghan soldier, who was limping badly and carrying a machine gun. "Are you hurt?" Kimberling asked.

The soldier, who didn't speak English, tapped his right knee and lifted his right pant leg to reveal a wooden leg. The strap that held it to his thigh had broken. So Kimberling threw him over his shoulder and carried him back to the Humvee.

Kimberling pulled out a roll of nylon rope called 550 cord, cut a lengthy piece, and used it to secure the wooden leg. The Afghan rolled his pant leg down, wiggled the wooden leg, and nodded with a big smile. In gratitude, he hugged Kimberling and kissed him on the cheek.

Handing the Afghan the rest of the cord, Kimberling said, "You're good to go, brother. Now, get back in the game."

Five of the six trucks were lined up near the mud shack. The troops inside the other vehicle, which was disabled by the IED, were pinned down by heavy fire. With King's leadership, rescuers fought their way to the truck and brought their comrades safely to the shack. The stricken vehicle, however, soon burst into flames.

King helped the troops set up a 50-foot semicircular perimeter. They had just one big machine gun, a 12.7-mm with only 150 rounds left. It was their last-ditch weapon. Set up in the back of an ANA Ford Ranger, it was manned by an Afghan sitting in an office chair that was bolted to the pickup's bed. The gunner was angry at Kimberling, who wouldn't let him shoot his weapon because they needed to conserve the ammunition. Despite enemy bullets flying from various directions, the pouting Afghan sat on the chair with his arms folded across his chest and his eyes glaring at Kimberling.

The tense battle and stifling heat were sapping the strength of everyone as streams of sweat dripped into their eyes and soaked their uniforms. The Americans shared what little water they had brought with the Afghans.

There was no time to rest. The militants tried to break through the troops' left flank, but were mowed down over open ground. Then the enemy tried the right flank by sneaking along a six-foot-deep creek bed 40 yards away. In response, the Americans led an assault team that ran to the edge of the creek bed and fired down, wiping out an estimated dozen insurgents.

As the Americans bounded back to the shack, Kimberling bent down to replace his magazine. Out of the corner of his eye, he spotted a militant poking his head around the wall of a small hut. Kimberling whipped out his pistol and fired two shots into the man's head.

When Kimberling returned to the mud shack inside the troops' perimeter, he saw Wenell holding a working Afghan cell phone. It was on a different cell network. "Where did you get that from?" Kimberling asked.

"One of the Afghan commanders had it, but never said anything until now."

Just then, an RPG exploded next to Wenell's head, bursting his eardrum so he could hardly hear and leaving him dazed. He handed Kimberling the phone and said, "Jake, you know how to call in air support. Get some planes in here."

Kimberling discovered the phone had no preprogrammed

numbers in it, so he scrolled through the directory of his own cell phone for the number of the major back at the base in Qalat and called him.

"Where are you and what are you doing?" the major demanded.

Kimberling gave a quick explanation, adding, "I got [enemy] contact all the way out to five hundred meters and as close as twenty-five meters. None of us are wounded. We were facing a force of thirty-five, but now it's seventy or greater."

Changing his tone completely, the major asked, "What do you need?"

Before he could answer, Kimberling saw the sulking Afghan machine gunner blazing away with his weapon at another Taliban charge from the creek bed. Kimberling dropped the phone, started shooting, and didn't stop until the enemy retreated.

When that skirmish ended, he picked the phone up off the ground, but it was beeping. The phone display said something in Pashto, one of the native languages of Afghanistan, so Kimberling called Hank over and asked, "What does this say?"

"It means the phone is out of minutes."

"You've got to be kidding me."

King poked his head around the corner and asked, "What's wrong, Jake?"

"The phone is out of minutes."

"You've got to be kidding me."

"Phil, go talk to the Afghans. Somebody must have a cell-phone card."

King hustled from one end of the perimeter to the other, collecting phone cards, and then hurried back to Kimberling, who was hunched in the doorway of the shack for cover. Scratching the numbers off the phone cards, King read them to Kimberling, who was punching them into the phone so they could get the minutes they needed to call for help.

Wenell came over and asked, "What's the hang-up, Jake?"

"The phone is out of minutes."

"You've got to be kidding me."

While the enemy began another attempt to close in on the troops, Hank brought an Afghan colonel to Kimberling and said, "Jake, the colonel has a special number you can use for free minutes in case of an emergency."

Kimberling rolled his eyes. Sarcastically he replied, "Really? Maybe an emergency will come up, you think? Does this not qualify? He couldn't have told us, like, I don't know, twenty minutes ago?"

Kimberling called the major again, but the reception was poor. Just as Kimberling began to give him the coordinates of their location, bullets cracked inches from his head and splintered the door, pelting his face with sharp slivers of wood.

"That hurt!" he moaned, clutching his head. Turning to an Afghan soldier nearby, he pointed to the shooter and said, "Hey, brother, kill him." The Afghan did just that with a burst of fire.

The call to the major was dropped again because the cell phone had lost its signal. So now Kimberling was forced to crouch down in the middle of the firefight with the phone cocked by his ear, trying to pick up a signal. As he strode by the trucks, the bulletproof windows were pelted by enemy fire. *Ping, ping, ping.*

Summoning his combat humor, King hollered, "Hey, Jake, I think someone is trying to kill you!"

"No kidding." *Ping, ping, ping.*

Switching to his earnest voice, King yelled, "Get over here!"

Kimberling scampered for cover, but he couldn't stay. He needed to move around to find a signal even if it meant being exposed. When he finally got a weak signal, he tried reaching the major, but without success. So he called the captain at the tactical operations center in Qalat and explained the situation. "Sir, I request emergency combat air support at this time."

He was told that two Dutch F-16s were taking off from Bagram Air Base 300 miles away. It would take at least 20 to 30 minutes before they would reach the area. Meanwhile, the Afghans were running out of ammo. But the small Afghan soldier, who had slapped the grenade away earlier in the fight, came up with a risky idea to ease the bullet shortage. He took off his combat gear but kept his automatic rifle. Then, under covering fire from his comrades, he sprinted across the open field toward an enemy position in the creek bed. He jumped down into it, shot the militants there, and gathered all their ammo. While enemy bullets from another position zinged past him, he dashed back to the perimeter to loud cheers from his comrades.

Even though the insurgents kept moving closer, the troops held their own while waiting for the planes. The firefight had reached the two-hour mark when the F-16s showed up. Unfortunately, the pilots couldn't find the troops and asked for a smoke grenade to mark the unit's position.

Handing King a smoke-grenade round, Kimberling said, "Phil, here's our last smoke. When I tell you, I want you to run out in the open and pop it. We'll cover you." King nodded and Kimberling yelled, "Go, go, go!"

Defying enemy fire, King charged out and launched the smoke grenade, which was quickly spotted by the pilots. But then they told Kimberling that before they could drop any bombs, they would have to do a show of force, which was required by the rules of engagement.

"Could we just skip that part?" he asked half jokingly. "Couldn't we just say we did it? This would be one time where cutting corners would be okay." When told no, he sighed and said, "Okay, make it low, make it loud, make it hurt."

The screeching jets swooped down from north to south only 50 feet off the ground—so close that Kimberling could see the pilots in the cockpits—and dropped flares on the enemy position in an effort to frighten them enough to flee.

The militants stopped shooting as if a switch had turned off the battle. Just as Kimberling wondered how long the silence would last, the firing picked up again. *Well, that didn't scare them*, he thought.

"I have no more smokes so I have no way to mark the target," he radioed the pilots. "I need you to drop the bombs right where I tell you. The target is due southwest from my position where the road turns and crosses over the creek next to two small busted-up houses. We're danger close."

Turning to King, he said, "Tell Mark to get everybody together and loaded into the trucks. When the bomb goes off, we'll bug out of here."

But now the troops were faced with a new dilemma. On the other side of the draw, another Taliban force of about 80 militants had arrived and was preparing to launch an attack from the nearby almond grove.

"Everybody in the trucks now!" Kimberling ordered. As the men peeled off toward their vehicles, their perimeter melted away. The troops then waited, hoping the bombs would drop before the larger enemy force rushed in. But the captain back at the tactical operations center—worried that civilians might be injured or killed in the village—called for a bomb damage assessment (BDA). Kimberling was ordered to stay behind until after the bombs were dropped.

He and an Afghan machine gunner took up a position on the knoll and tried to hold off the advancing enemy. Kimberling was gripping the cell phone in one hand and firing with the other while his comrades were shooting over his head from the backs of their trucks.

Suddenly, an RPG blew up several yards in front of the two men, and then a second exploded much closer. Kimberling gripped the machine gunner's shoulder and said, "The next one is not going to miss. We need to go!" He shouted in the cell phone, "Captain, I can't stay here. I have to move out now!" Dodging enemy fire, the two raced 150 yards down the road and across open ground to the waiting trucks.

Because Kimberling couldn't conduct a BDA, the bombing run was called off. "At least have the planes do another pass," he urged the captain. Before he received an answer, the phone died.

The trucks roared to life and zoomed toward the valley as the troops fought their way through creek beds and past alleyways. Eventually the convoy made it across the river and back onto Route 1 and relative safety.

When they finally stopped and took a break, the joyous

Afghans danced in celebration and hugged the three Americans. "You fought like lions," marveled one Afghan officer. "You didn't abandon us."

"No matter what, we were going to fight with you from start to finish," Kimberling told them. "And the best thing is, we didn't have a single casualty."

It was later determined by the military that the Americans and their 35 Afghan comrades had faced an enemy force of an estimated 300 Taliban and al-Qaeda fighters, of which at least 25 were killed.

The Americans' reputation with the ANA and ANP soared. *We can do no wrong in their eyes*, Kimberling thought on the way back to the base. But after they returned, the three airmen were given a tongue-lashing — by the base's cook. He was furious because they had given the dehydrated and tired Afghans his entire stash of Gatorade.

The battle at Ebrahimkhel was the largest ground-to-ground firefight involving air force personnel since the Vietnam War in 1968.

For his actions that day, Staff Sergeant Jason "Jake" Kimberling was awarded a Bronze Star with Valor and the Army Commendation Medal. He was also named the 2008 recipient of the Colonel Billy Jack Carter Award, the highest individual honor bestowed by the air force's security forces.

"Sergeant Kimberling is an air force combat hero," said Colonel Thomas Laffey, 366th Mission Support Group commander.

Said Kimberling, "I don't think I did anything special. I went out there and did my job."

Senior Airman Phillip King was also awarded a Bronze Star with Valor for his heroism that day. Echoing his fellow airman, King said the intense fight was "just another day on the job."

In the Chaos of Combat

TECH SERGEANT MARK DeCORTE

U.S. Air Force Tech Sergeant Mark DeCorte could feel the adrenaline pumping through his body. It was the same sensation he always experienced whenever he was ready to put his life on the line to save a critically wounded soldier.

Through his night vision goggles (NVGs), the medic looked out the open door of the HH-60 Pave Hawk helicopter and saw a raging firefight nearby and then a fireball from a 2,000-pound bomb. Seconds from now, he would have to bound out of the chopper, run through a kill zone covered on three sides by enemy forces, find the wounded soldier in the bedlam of battle in the black of night, and give emergency aid. Then DeCorte would have to carry him past the enemy to the waiting helicopter and keep him alive during the flight back to the base for a chance at life-saving surgery. Adding to the stress: The chopper might not be there waiting for them.

If anyone could pull it off, it was DeCorte. He was one of only three airmen handpicked as the first combat flight medics in a joint Army–Air Force experiment that was classified at the time. Each was assigned as the solo armed medic on specially outfitted helicopter gunships. In a job that combined compassion with aggression, DeCorte was a member of a five-man crew that provided air support for those on the ground and tracked movements in battle. Among the 12-year veteran's responsibilities were to resupply troops with weapons, ammo, and water; help rescue downed airmen; and treat and medevac the wounded — all during the chaos of combat.

On this particular nighttime mission in 2006, DeCorte, of Thirty-third Expeditionary Combat Rescue Squadron, was at his customary spot in the back of the cramped cabin of the Pave Hawk, behind the gunner, flight engineer, pilot, and copilot. The heavily armed chopper was hovering near ground troops who were attacking an enemy compound when he received word that an RPG had struck a soldier near the groin and blown off his legs. The medic was told that the victim was lying somewhere on a road near the compound. Time was running out before the soldier bled to death.

While stuffing his medical bag with extra supplies, DeCorte slipped some tourniquets around his ankles so they would be easier to reach when he needed them. DeCorte glanced outside to keep tabs on his "situational awareness." He wanted to get his bearings — a sense for what was happening in the battle below and a better understanding of the locations of the friendly and enemy forces.

As the Pave Hawk set down, the whirring rotor blades kicked up sand in a blinding brownout that fanned out about 50 yards. DeCorte couldn't see anything in the swirling dust, not even with his NVGs. He had standing orders not to leave the rotor area, but most times he had to leave — and this was one of those times. He knew the risks. If the chopper should come under attack, it would have to take off without him, because it was an expensive piece of machinery, and there were four other lives at stake.

"Medic off com!" he shouted before disconnecting the communications cord of his headset from the helicopter. He couldn't spare precious seconds while waiting for the brownout to clear. He ran through the flying dust and emerged in an oxen-plowed field ribbed by rows of three-foot-tall crests of dirt.

In times like this, a soldier relies on all his senses for survival. But DeCorte was without one of them — hearing. His helmet had built-in earmuffs to quell the noise of the chopper. If he removed the muffs to listen for the enemy or an incoming mortar round, he wouldn't be able to see much in the dark, because his helmet also had built-in NVGs. He chose to keep his helmet on during his mad dash across the field. Through his NVGs, which made everything appear in shades of green, his eyes were constantly moving as they scanned for the enemy, exposed IEDs, and safe footing.

To his left, he noticed a tree line teeming with dark shadows. *Taliban fighters!* His instincts told him to rush back to the helicopter and save himself. But his courage and training refused to listen. He had a life to save. *Don't dwell on the bad guys*, he thought. *Just run.* Despite the heavy gear he carried, he bolted for the next field, barely aware of occasional streaks of light from enemy fire. *Don't pay attention to them. Keep running.* He didn't want to think about what would happen if he were captured. His survival training had included time spent in a simulated prisoner-of-war camp. It wasn't pleasant. But it would seem like a resort compared to being captured, tortured, and killed by the Taliban.

When DeCorte reached the next field, he dove into tall grass. Then, hunching over, he scurried onto a hardened dirt road and searched in the dark for the wounded man as the firefight continued. After a few anxious minutes, he found the fallen soldier on the road, unconscious and close to death from massive blood loss.

DeCorte deliberately relaxed, releasing the nervous tension that had built up during his dangerous run across the battlefield. If he remained too hyper, he wouldn't be able to think clearly or feel the patient's pulse, because the medic's own heart would be pumping too hard. *I have to calm down and focus on this guy, or he's not going to live.*

When the medic arrived, the victim was lying on his back, surrounded by soldiers who were frantically trying to stem the bleeding by using bandages and tourniquets from their individual first-aid kits. But they were so intent on dealing with the injury that they hadn't looked at the soldier's face. That was the first thing DeCorte did. He saw that the victim wasn't breathing because he was choking on his own vomit. Reacting quickly, DeCorte flipped him over so he was facedown, picked him up by the belt and collar, and dropped him over the medic's knee.

As bizarre as this action looked to the other soldiers, it worked. DeCorte had cleared the patient's airway.

At this point, hearing became more important than seeing in the dark, so DeCorte took off his helmet because he needed to hear the soldier breathe. The medic placed the victim at the side of the road and gave CPR until he heard him coughing and groaning. *Good, good! He's breathing again.*

DeCorte tried to forget the pain in his own back. He was wearing body armor, a rucksack, aircrew gear, ground-pounding gear, survival gear, and medical bags. Together they weighed so much that when he leaned forward, his back muscles strained to keep him from falling on top of his patient.

After resuscitating the soldier, DeCorte worked hard to stabilize him. The medic remained so focused that he barely paid attention to the sights or sounds of combat, although twice he instinctively shielded the patient from raining debris caused by close secondary explosions.

It'll be safer for us to stay with the troops until this firefight is over instead of taking him out in the open, the medic thought. *But if I don't move him now, this guy isn't going to make it.*

The seconds were ticking off the "golden hour," the period of time following a traumatic injury when it's believed the victim's chances for survival are the greatest with prompt emergency care.

As soon as DeCorte was ready to move him, the medic put his helmet back on so he could once again see in the dark through his NVGs. When there was a lull in the fighting, the soldiers near him remained prone, their weapons aimed at the same Taliban force that DeCorte had slipped past minutes earlier. Because he had lost his situational awareness while treating his patient, he didn't have a full picture of the firefight. *If anyone shoots while I'm running, my patient and I will probably die, because we'll be out in the middle of it all. But I can't wait. I have to take that chance.*

DeCorte punched one of the soldiers in the arm and said, "I need you to cover us." Not hearing any response, the medic decided to chance it, anyway. Carrying his patient, the stocky five-foot nine-inch medic began hustling across 75 yards of open space past the militants. He was living up to his call sign and nickname — "Tank."

As the medic ran, his eyes darted from the ground to the enemy's position in the tree line off his right shoulder. Every few seconds, he glanced forward, hoping to see the waiting helicopter. *Where's the chopper? I don't see it! They didn't leave, did they? Did I lose my bearings? Should I turn more to my left?* He altered his course slightly. His legs were beginning to burn from hurdling the plowed mounds while carrying all that extra weight. His body began tensing from the worry that he had been left behind. *It's got to be around here somewhere. . . . Wait. . . . Is that it? . . . Yes!* When he reached the Pave Hawk, he slid his patient onto the floor of the chopper and dived in, yelling to the crew, "Let's go! Let's go! Let's go!"

As the chopper lifted off, DeCorte told the pilot, "Go full speed." Wanting him to alert the base to get the operating room ready, the medic added, "Call in and tell them to stand up the OR." He tightened the tourniquets and inserted IVs into the soldier to control the pain and replenish some of the lost blood.

After the Pave Hawk landed, DeCorte off-loaded the patient and brought him straight through the entry of the OR. As he turned the soldier over to the waiting surgical team, he shouted out everything he had done to treat the victim.

There was no time for discussion, no time to catch his breath, no time for a bathroom break. The battle wasn't over yet, which meant he and his crew needed to get back in the air. On his way out the door, he hurried to the medical-supply cabinet. Replacing what he had used on his patient, DeCorte swatted the supplies he needed off the shelves and into his helmet, which was cradled in his arm.

The helicopter was still running when he jumped back in. After taking a few deep breaths, the medic suddenly was gripped by an uneasy sensation. He was beginning to feel all the fear and stress that he had blocked out during his life-saving mission.

But he buried those emotions once again when the crew was informed that a soldier needed immediate help after a deadly snake bit him. While the Pave Hawk changed course to an area not under attack, DeCorte forced himself to forget about the legless soldier, the Taliban, and the RPG explosions. He had to concentrate on the next guy he needed to save.

When DeCorte arrived at the scene, he assessed the soldier, who was nearly unconscious, in terrible pain, and having trouble breathing. He had been bitten in the ankle by a pit viper, whose poison can kill its victim within an hour or two without proper emergency aid. Thanks to the medic's fast treatment, the crisis passed. "You're going to make it," DeCorte told him.

After the crew returned to base, the copilot revealed to DeCorte, "Tonight was my first medevac, and I didn't like it because I have a phobia about hospitals and injuries. I almost got sick from the smell of blood back there. I'm not sure I can handle seeing all that blood and guts."

DeCorte wanted to change the copilot's attitude. So the medic took him to the surgical tent where they watched the last few minutes of the surgery on the critically wounded soldier they had brought in earlier that night. Although the victim lost both legs, the doctors felt confident that he would live.

While witnessing the operation, the copilot squirmed, repeatedly closed his eyes, and nearly threw up. When it was over, he asked DeCorte, "Why did you make me watch that?"

"You need to see for yourself that you helped save a guy's life. I may be the medic, but you flew me there and back. You need to take ownership of this life-saving effort and understand how big a difference you made for this soldier."

After a moment of reflection, the copilot nodded and declared, "I'm beginning to get it now."

"Good, because you *need* to get it," said DeCorte, slapping him on the back.

DeCorte couldn't have been anything but a combat flight medic. It was in his genes. His father, mother, and uncle served in the air force as medical sergeants. His brother was an air force sergeant (although not a medic). Even DeCorte's wife, Lorretta, who was deployed to Iraq during this time, was an air force medic.

Possessing a passion for his work, DeCorte was the perfect choice for the first test of the combat flight medic experiment in Afghanistan. Throughout his five-month deployment, he was on call 24 hours a day, seven days a week, never knowing what perilous or critical situation he would face next.

Over and over, he was called on to resupply troops on an active battlefield. Once, during a vicious nighttime firefight west of Kabul, a small American unit was trapped in a valley, taking fire from two positions. The men were down to two magazines each when DeCorte arrived after a four-hour flight. Braving enemy fire, he and a crewman lugged three body bags full of ammo, replacement weapons, and five-gallon jugs of water. The fresh supplies helped turn the tide for the Americans.

Hardly a week went by when DeCorte didn't have to deal with an unusual medical crisis. One time, while his gunship was escorting a convoy of Chinook helicopters, a chopper made a forced landing that caused serious damage. DeCorte was on the ground within a minute. He dashed inside the copter and pulled out the flight engineer, who was blinded by hydraulic fluid that had sprayed on his face. The medic cut open two bags of IV fluid and dumped them in the victim's eyes. Then DeCorte carried him to the Pave Hawk, hooked an IV bag to an oxygen mask, and slapped it over the victim's eyes, flushing them out. Thanks to the medic's spur-of-the-moment creativity, the flight engineer didn't suffer any eye damage and was returned to flying status later that night.

In his job, DeCorte expected the unexpected. One night about 2 A.M., the crew prepared to lift off from their base in Kandahar to medevac two soldiers who were wounded in a firefight about 25 miles away. Moments before the flight, the pilot told DeCorte, "Just got a report that there are multiple casualties. The Taliban had attacked our foot soldiers with small-arms fire before running away. Two of our guys were wounded. The rest of the troops chased after the Taliban and were joined by a mechanized unit.

But they ran right into an RPG ambush that pretty much disabled the entire convoy. I don't know how many are injured, but it's a lot more than two."

DeCorte began mentally preparing himself. Whenever he was about to enter a combat zone, he felt an initial wave of fear, which was a normal reaction to an abnormal situation. But he also felt a surge of excitement at the chance to save a life. Or in this case, many lives.

When the Pave Hawk reached the area, DeCorte saw several army vehicles on fire. Because of the danger of another possible ambush, the chopper landed 150 yards away near a sprawling field.

Every time DeCorte hopped off the helicopter, he would decide whether or not to go off com, but he never hesitated in making his decision. This time he did. The area looked suspiciously like a minefield. Afghanistan is one of the world's most heavily land-mined countries because of previous wars, including a nine-year conflict with the Russians in the 1980s. Concealed inches below the surface in fields like this one could be countless IEDs planted by the Taliban, antipersonnel mines buried by al-Qaeda militants, and old antitank mines left from the Russian invasion.

"Can we get any closer?" DeCorte asked the pilot.

"No, it's the best we can do."

After a moment's thought, DeCorte said, "Medic off com!" He unhitched his link to the helicopter and started running, but carefully. He kept his eyes on the ground, looking for every strange divot and every unnatural little mound that might indicate a land mine. *There's a divot. . . . There's a mound. . . . Another one . . .*

That seems suspicious. . . . This sure looks like a minefield.

After sidestepping his way to the middle of the field, he stopped to catch his breath. He gazed ahead at the flames licking the burning trucks. *The bad guys are probably still around. If they plan another ambush, I'll just have to run right through them.* Not seeing any signs of the enemy, he took off his helmet and listened. All he heard was the droning of the helicopter's engine.

For one brief moment, he treated himself to a guilty pleasure — a quick glance at the sparkling, diamond-dusted sky. *Gee, the stars are so beautiful.* They gave him a certain peace of mind, an otherworldly comfort as if they were watching over him. *Okay, you better get going.* He put on his helmet and took one more peek at the stars, this time through his NVGs.

He picked up the pace. But, still wary of the suspected land mines, DeCorte accepted the likelihood that the next step could be his last. Because his missions were always so dangerous, he had come to terms with being killed. He had all his personal effects in order, had written a will, and had penned letters to his wife and four children to be read after his death. Every day in country was a day he knew he could die . . . and he was okay with that. His acceptance meant he could concentrate on his job and not worry about anything else.

When he reached the burning convoy, he saw walking wounded everywhere. Knowing he couldn't treat everybody, he announced, "Some of you must help yourselves. Those who aren't hurt should pair up with those who are." He barked instructions to several soldiers who were trying to treat their injured comrades.

He started doing triage, looking for those who needed aid immediately, those whose injuries weren't life threatening, and those who were beyond help. His quick assessment: *No one is going to die tonight.* But there were many soldiers suffering from serious wounds.

DeCorte identified five for medevac. *I can't leave behind anyone who's too injured to defend himself,* he thought.

He selected one soldier with a head wound; two with severe burns to the back and head; one with shrapnel wounds to the face and neck; and, the most seriously injured of the group, a soldier whose hand was blown off. But getting the five to the helicopter would be a challenge, because it meant guiding them across the potential minefield in pitch blackness.

After putting a tourniquet on the soldier who lost his hand, the medic gave him an IV, but he kept losing consciousness. DeCorte would have to carry him back.

"Can't you take more with you?" one of the wounded soldiers asked.

"I feel bad leaving the others behind," said the medic, "but the helicopter has room for only two patients."

"But there are five of us."

"I know. Don't worry. Leave that to me." *Just how am I going to fit all of them in there?*

The medic couldn't fret about that now. His main concern was getting them to the helicopter. While carrying the unconscious soldier, DeCorte lined up the other four and said, "Hold on to the guy in front of you, because you won't be able to see a thing in the dark. I'm the only one with NVGs, so I'll be in the lead. Follow directly behind me and don't stray."

Without any cover fire or escorts, DeCorte and the walking wounded slowly headed across the hazardous stretch toward the waiting chopper. With each step, the tension in the medic's neck and shoulders tightened. He was worried for his injured comrades. *It's one thing if I get blown up; it's another if I take them to their deaths, too.*

To ease his burden, a couple of the wounded helped carry the unconscious soldier and assisted one another the best they could. The going was slow and deliberate, and it took much longer than he thought it would to get back. He sacrificed speed to concentrate on avoiding any land mines and looking out for possible ambushes. He didn't think about anything else until they neared the helicopter. By then, some of the men were in terrible pain and straggling. "We're almost there," he said. DeCorte began working out a plan in his mind to cram everyone into the four-by-six-foot space that was designed to accommodate only two patients.

When they made it to the Pave Hawk, DeCorte slid the unconscious soldier onto the floor, helped two others get in, and had them curl up against the far door. The medic climbed in next and then grabbed the chest harnesses of the last two and pulled them into the aircraft one at a time. They both landed on top of him. After the gunner closed the door, the pair leaned against it in fetal positions.

With two on his left and two on his right, DeCorte sat in the middle, facing forward toward the unconscious soldier. The medic was in reach of all five and mentally labeled them *A*, *B*, *C*, *D*, and *E*. Everything in the cabin was blacked out because lights inside the low-flying helicopter could give its position away to the enemy. In order to see what he was doing, he used a little green light built into his helmet's microphone that he turned on with his tongue.

He also used a green penlight to repeatedly check each person's vital signs and examine their injuries. *I keep finding more wounds that I hadn't seen the first time.* During the flight, he bandaged new wounds and adjusted the tourniquet. Whenever his back was turned to the unconscious soldier, the medic gave him a little nudge to make him groan. As long as the patient was making a sound, he was breathing.

Instead of writing the patients' names and vital signs on a piece of paper to give the emergency room staff upon arrival, he used a Sharpie pen to jot the information on his patients' arms and clothes throughout the flight.

Shortly before the chopper landed, DeCorte looked into the eyes of the four conscious soldiers to make sure they were still alert. "Give me a signal if you're doing okay," he said. They all gave him a thumbs-up.

Later when DeCorte learned that all five of his patients were doing well, it was his turn to give a thumbs-up. After each mission, that was all he ever wanted.

While based in Kandahar, Mark DeCorte, who was promoted to master sergeant, flew on 63 missions as a combat flight medic, and was credited with saving 36 lives.

His leadership and actions on the battlefield earned him the 2006 Expeditionary Non-Commissioned Officer of the Year award.

"If I were deploying again and could take only one other airman with me, the choice would be easy—Mark DeCorte,"

said Colonel Jim Sterling, Fifth Medical Support Squadron commander. "You know he'll be there for you when the bottom drops out under any circumstances. He'll ensure the mission is complete and make sure you return alive. It doesn't get any better than that."

From February to June of 2006, DeCorte and the other two specially selected combat flight medics — Master Sergeant Scott Curran and Tech Sergeant Shawn Bendixson (who have since been promoted to senior master sergeant and master sergeant respectively) — collectively saved the lives of 138 soldiers and Afghans who would have otherwise died. However, the army-air force experiment that the trio had started was phased out because the military determined it was just too risky.

The Ambush at Afghanya

SPECIALIST GREGORY "SCOTT" RUSKE

As his small squad walked into the village of Afghanya, Army Reserve Specialist Gregory "Scott" Ruske started getting an uneasy feeling.

He had been in country for nearly eight months and had participated in many of these missions, known as "presence patrols." Soldiers would enter areas unannounced to let the locals — and, more important, the Taliban — know that the military was there to offer help and protection. Often the people would emerge from their mud huts and wave at the troops. Children would laugh and tag along with the patrol for a few minutes, hoping someone would toss them a piece of candy.

But not here. *This place has a strange vibe to it,* Ruske thought. There were no friendly nods, no pleasant smiles. *Too many dudes are staring at us with mean eyes, like they're angry and wish us harm.* He had seen that look before — usually from Taliban supporters.

The scene was ominously similar to his first taste of close combat six months earlier when he was on a presence patrol. The troops were riding in a convoy through a village populated by people who made it obvious by their cold gazes that the Americans were not welcome. Moments later, the villagers disappeared . . . and the Taliban attacked. As Ruske was bolting from his vehicle to take the fight to the enemy, an RPG narrowly missed him and slammed into a tree a few feet away and exploded. Feeling his chest vibrate from the blast's shock wave, he yelled to his battle buddy, half in jest, "Holy smokes! They're seriously trying to kill us!"

Months of firefights, patrols, and mortar attacks had made the 28-year-old Army Reserve soldier from Colorado Springs, Colorado, combat-hardened. He had been shot at so many times that he could tell how close a bullet was to his head by the sound it made. A crack or snap was a few inches; a zip or hiss, a few feet. Drawing from his experience and training, he knew what to do in most any crisis situation. He also developed a heightened sense of impending danger.

On this otherwise picture-perfect day, April 21, 2008, he sensed danger.

Ruske was attached to the Pennsylvania National Guard's Third Battalion, 103rd Armor Regiment, working under the 101st Airborne Division. Carrying an M203 grenade launcher attached to his M16 rifle, Ruske was walking at the rear of the patrol, which was made up of nine fellow members of Third Platoon, Alpha Company, Task Force Gladiator, Combined Joint Task Force 101.

Joining them were two ANP officers—Syed and Abdul (not their real names)—and an interpreter.

Forced to leave their gun trucks because the road had become impassable in the harsh terrain of Kapisa Province, the soldiers had entered Afghanya on foot. Through the interpreter, the local elders were told that the Americans were capable of showing up anywhere, at any time, in the region to rout the Taliban. Judging from the icy expressions on the villagers' faces, Ruske could see they weren't impressed, that they obviously sided with the Taliban.

As the soldiers hiked out of Afghanya toward the next village, they entered a narrow valley of farmland bordered by mountains on the left and rocky hills on the right. Ruske's uneasiness swelled. He nervously tapped the playing card—a king of hearts—that he always kept for good luck in the band of his helmet. His eyes were constantly in motion, looking for any signs of the Taliban.

The soldiers were walking past a two-family walled compound when—just as he suspected—they were ambushed. Long bursts of fire from RPK and PKM machine guns, AK-47s, and grenade blasts shattered the quiet. From the front of the patrol came screams of shock and pain and shouts of "Cover!" The Americans dropped to the ground and began shooting back.

Ruske had experienced enough firefights to get his combat routine down pat: Head for cover and then lay down heavy fire. He bolted for the corner of a wall and began shooting his M16 and launching grenades into the side of the nearest hill.

Seeing that several of his comrades were firing from prone positions on the open ground in a shallow ditch, he hollered, "You guys are in a bad spot. Get up and pull back. I'll cover you." He jumped out from behind the wall and fired at the enemy, allowing the soldiers to dash for safety behind the compound's wall. Then he ducked behind it, too.

The soldiers kicked down the door to the compound and streamed into a courtyard, using its two-foot-thick mud-and-rock walls for cover. The houses inside the compound were searched to make sure there were no militants.

In a typical Taliban ambush, a small group launches a hit-and-run attack. After engaging an American patrol for a few minutes, they flee. The Americans call in air support and then chase after the enemy. But within minutes, Ruske sensed that this was not an ordinary ambush. He couldn't tell how many Taliban there were, but based on the amount of heavy fire, he knew one thing: *There are a whole lot more of them than there are of us. And they aren't running away.* In fact, as the firefight raged on, Taliban fighters maneuvered their way toward the Americans in an attempt to surround them.

What Ruske and his comrades didn't know until later was that the patrol had, by its very presence in the village, disrupted a meeting of high-ranking Taliban officials. According to the military's after-action report, the patrol of ten Americans and three Afghans was facing an estimated 100 Taliban fighters.

When Ruske took his eyes off the enemy positions, he saw that the two Afghan policemen, who were at the front of the patrol, had been shot in the opening salvo. Abdul had fallen to his knees after taking several bullets in the arm, but he managed to get up and scramble for cover.

But Syed lay flat on his back and wasn't moving. His blue-gray uniform was turning crimson from the waist down. *Poor man*, Ruske thought. *He was lit up pretty good.* Like the rest of the Americans, Ruske assumed Syed was dead.

Of all the members of the ANP, Syed was Ruske's favorite. They had worked together several times, either on a patrol or at the little police checkpoint that Syed often manned. Through an interpreter, Ruske had friendly chats with the tall, thin officer with the salt-and-pepper hair and goatee to match. Ruske was impressed with Syed for his pleasant manner and positive attitude. Syed would always help the Americans in any way he could. In appreciation, Ruske would give him any extra food like an MRE (a packaged, ready-to-eat meal) or other supplies.

He wasn't even supposed to be with us today, Ruske thought. The Americans had expected an ANP squad to join them earlier in the day, but it never showed up. Syed had asked his commander if he and Abdul could go with the troops, but the commander had said no. The two policemen went anyway. Now one was badly wounded and the other was presumed dead.

The Americans helped Abdul to an area behind a wall that enclosed the compound's orchard. There, he was treated for multiple wounds to his arm. Even though the soldiers didn't have a medic with them, some were trained as combat lifesavers. They carried basic medical gear and knew how to use field dressings, IVs, splints, and tourniquets to keep a wounded person alive until more qualified medical help was available.

While Abdul was being treated, the Americans were desperately trying to hold off the militants. Because the soldiers were outnumbered ten to one, the team leader radioed for air support and a QRF — a quick reaction force — to assist them. But no one knew how long it would take for help to arrive.

Inching their way toward the besieged compound, the insurgents had a tactical advantage because they were on higher ground and had better shooting angles than the Americans. As bullets flew from all directions, Ruske ran over to his squad leader, Sergeant First Class David Baltrusaitis, and said, "I want to go up on the roof and get a good look. Maybe we can attack the enemy from up there."

"Okay. Take a couple of men with you."

Ruske, Specialist Eric Segraves, who was his battle buddy, and Captain Jason Monholland climbed up a rickety ladder made of twigs and sticks. When they reached the roof, they found their view was blocked by tall trees and another wall. "This isn't a good fighting position for us," said Ruske. "Let's get out of here."

As he watched the captain start down the wobbly ladder, Ruske thought, *I don't think that ladder is safe enough to . . .*

Suddenly, the surface of the roof exploded all around him. *They're shooting at us!* Monholland scrambled down the ladder, but not Segraves. He leaped off the roof, landing hard with an impact made worse by all his heavy gear. Before Ruske could reach the ladder, he felt a stabbing pain in his lower left hip and his lower back, as if someone had snapped him with a giant rubber band. He dove for a corner of the roof wall to get out of the enemy's sight. After pressing his gloved hand against his hip, he saw blood on his palm. *They actually managed to shoot me*, he thought. "Dude!" he shouted to Segraves. "I've been hit!"

"Can you move?"

"Yeah. I need you to cover me so I can get down off this roof."

As Segraves provided suppressive fire aimed at the nearest

hill, Ruske scrambled down the ladder. "Going on the roof probably wasn't a smart idea," he told Segraves.

"How badly are you hurt?" Segraves asked him.

"My hip is numb," Ruske replied, poking it gently. "It's not too bad. I can stick it out and stay in the fight."

Staff Sergeant Bill Sampson, who had treated Abdul, examined Ruske's wound and said, "It appears pretty clean. Looks like the round hit nothing but meat. You're lucky."

The enemy bullet had punched through a rifle magazine attached to the left side of Ruske's belt and glanced off two rounds. Missing his body armor by half an inch, the bullet had traveled into his hip and, without nicking any bones, arteries, or organs, exited out his lower back. After Sampson put a field dressing on the wounds, Ruske picked up his weapon, hustled back to a wall, and began shooting.

His eye caught movement on the ground about 50 yards away. Syed, whom everyone thought was dead, was trying to crawl out of the kill zone.

"He's alive!" Ruske shouted.

Grimacing in agony and fear, Syed was clawing at the ground on his belly, leaving behind a bloody trail. He was working his way slowly along a shallow ditch that Ruske could tell wasn't deep enough to provide any meaningful cover. Bullets were kicking up dirt just inches from his head. *They're deliberately taking potshots at him even though he's no longer a threat to them. That's just sick!*

Turning to Segraves, Ruske said, "Man, we've got to get to this guy before they kill him. We can't just leave him there. He's one of us. He's an ally."

"Okay, dude. I'm with you," said Segraves, who was usually willing to go along with Ruske's plans, no matter how risky.

Ruske talked it over with Sergeant First Class David Hopkins, the squad leader, who was at the corner of the compound. Hopkins said, "I'll pop out and provide cover fire while you and Segraves run out and get him."

Specialist Walter Reed, the patrol's SAW (squad automatic weapon) gunner, was called over. Ruske pointed to a spot where enemy fire was coming from and said, "Reed, on my count, unload your drum and give me a nice Z-pattern on those hills over there."

Hopkins told Ruske and Segraves to leave their weapons behind. "In case something bad should happen to you two, I don't want the enemy to get your weapons," Hopkins explained. "Besides, you need to keep both your hands free."

"Do you have anything to defend yourself?" Segraves asked Ruske.

"A pocketknife."

"Oh, yeah, that'll be a big help," Segraves cracked.

Trying to slow down his anxiety-fueled breathing, Ruske shouted to Hopkins and Reed, "Okay, on the count of three . . . One . . . two . . . three!"

Ruske and Segraves charged into the kill zone as Reed and Hopkins jumped out from behind their cover and fired nonstop. The only thing Ruske thought as he made his mad dash was, *I hope this works.* He heard the raw bursts from Reed's SAW but nothing else. He was totally focused on grabbing Syed and getting him out of harm's way.

As Reed and Hopkins ripped off more than 200 rounds, Ruske and Segraves reached Syed. They each gripped a wrist and began dragging him back. Above the din from Reed's SAW, Ruske heard the frightening cracking and snapping of the enemy bullets. *I hope I don't get hit again. That would be a bummer.*

Rounds hissing all around them, the two soldiers towed Syed all the way into the outer courtyard. "We did it!" shouted Ruske.

He saw from the bullet holes in Syed's bloody uniform that the Afghan had been hit several times in the back and in the legs. As Ruske picked him up by the legs and Segraves by the arms to carry him to a more secure area, Syed's left leg folded the wrong way and he let out a scream. "Holy smokes!" gasped Ruske. "The bullets have nearly cut off his leg!"

The two soldiers brought him inside the walled-in orchard area and then tore off his pant legs so they could examine and treat his wounds. Ruske spotted an AK-47 round inside one of the discarded pant legs. He picked up the bullet and gave it to Syed. "Here, this might make a neat souvenir for you," Ruske told him.

Syed glared at the bloody round and flung it away.

"I guess you're not in the mood for a souvenir," said Ruske.

The soldiers splinted his shattered leg and put a tourniquet on it to restrict the blood loss. Syed lay on the ground, moaning in pain. The interpreter got a blanket from the owner of the house and wrapped it around Syed.

Ruske went back to the fight, which was turning grimmer by the minute. The swarming militants were advancing closer to the compound. Although American planes circled over the area, serious communications problems between the patrol and the pilots prevented any aerial attacks. The pilots weren't allowed to shoot if they couldn't make direct contact with the troops on the ground because of the risk of friendly-fire casualties. Even though Ruske shot off smoke grenades to mark the patrol's position, that wasn't good enough.

Adding to the soldiers' woes, the QRF got ambushed on its way to help them and was now bottled up in a firefight outside of town.

"We're on our own," Ruske told Segraves.

"It's starting to get a little iffy. Reed is getting low on SAW rounds, and the rest of us are getting low on ammo, too."

"We have to conserve and make every bullet count."

Ruske was too busy holding back the enemy to pay much attention to the increasing pain in his hip and back. The sting was made worse by his body armor, which rubbed the wounds with every movement he made.

During a pause in the fighting, Ruske dropped back into the orchard area, sat down with Syed, and held his hand. Every 30 seconds Syed would start shivering uncontrollably. *I'm scared for him, and I don't think he's going to live much longer*, thought Ruske, who tried to mask his worries with a smile. Hoping to calm Syed, Ruske talked to him in a comforting voice: "You're going to make it. We'll get you out of here and patch you up. Just hold on." Even though Ruske knew that Syed didn't understand the words, the soldier hoped that Syed still got the message.

When Ruske left to fight some more, he figured that when he returned, Syed would be dead. But to his surprise, on his next visit,

Syed was still alive. This time, the interpreter was there to translate. While enemy rounds occasionally cracked overhead, Ruske gave Syed a running account of the battle. "Not to worry," said Ruske. "The enemy won't overrun us. Help is on the way. Everything is going to be okay." At least that was what Ruske hoped.

Eventually, the QRF fought through its ambush and arrived to help turn the tide. Soon the patrol was bolstered by members of the Army Special Forces, 101st Airborne Division, French Foreign Legion, ANA, and ANP.

The battle wore on for nearly six grueling hours before the Taliban—with most of its fighters dead or wounded—gave up and fled into the hills.

Other than Ruske and the two Afghans, there were no casualties. The soldiers kicked down a door in the orchard wall and used it as a litter for Syed. Then members of the ANP carried him to a landing zone where he and Abdul were helicoptered to the hospital at nearby Bagram Air Base.

Although Ruske was in pain and blood was seeping through his uniform, he limped back to the gun trucks with the rest of the patrol. "Despite everything that went wrong today, we did all right," he said to Segraves. "We managed to bring everyone home alive. That makes it a good day."

Later, after examining Ruske's wound, a Special Forces medic told him, "It's more serious than you think." A helicopter flew the soldier to Bagram for further treatment. The staff took his bloody clothes—including his favorite T-shirt and a belt with a bullet hole in it—and burned them.

From the hospital, Ruske called his family. "Mom, I have some good news and some bad news," he told her. "I've been shot, but I'm fine. It was just meat." He explained what happened and assured her there was no reason to be upset. "I'm in the hospital, drinking Mountain Dew. It's all good. It's all good."

After getting stitched up, Ruske stayed in Bagram for a few days, so he visited Syed in the hospital. The soldier found him lying in bed with his damaged leg in a cast. The doctor said that Syed would walk again, but that Abdul might have permanent nerve damage in his arm.

During Ruske's visit, there was no talk about how he had risked his own life to help save Syed's. It was clear to the soldier that Syed never knew who dragged him to safety. And that was just fine with Ruske.

After finishing his tour of duty in Afghanistan, a fully recovered Scott Ruske, who was promoted to sergeant and given a Purple Heart, returned to his civilian job as a juvenile-corrections officer in Denver, Colorado.

For his actions during that tense April 2008 firefight, Ruske was awarded the Silver Star by Lieutenant General Jack C. Stultz, chief of the Army Reserve. Stultz said, "Sergeant Ruske's actions demonstrated commitment, selfless service, and personal courage. This warrior-citizen is a great American hero who put his life on hold — and on the line — to defend our country and our freedoms. The sacrifices Army Reserve soldiers and their families make every day make a difference in people's lives."

After the ceremony, Ruske said, "I don't consider myself a hero. I was just an ordinary guy put in an extraordinary situation. I reacted based on my upbringing, training, and compassion. And, thankfully, it worked out in the end.

"I had help the whole time. It's not like it was just me. None of it would have been possible without Walter Reed and Eric Segraves helping me."

Segraves was awarded the Army Commendation Medal with Valor.

Praising Ruske, Sergeant First Class David Baltrusaitis said, *"I think of him as a hero. He risked his life for a guy he barely knew. It says a lot about him personally. Absolutely, he's one of the bravest men I've fought with."*

The "Fire-and-Forget" Guys

CAPTAIN SHEFFIELD FORD III,
MASTER SERGEANT THOM MAHOLIC,
STAFF SERGEANT MATTHEW BINNEY,
STAFF SERGEANT JOSEPH FUERST III,
SERGEANT FIRST CLASS ABRAM HERNANDEZ

Heavily armed Taliban were showing up in remote farming villages in Panjawai District, Kandahar Province, with an ultimatum to the locals: Support us or leave your homes and fields. It was the middle of harvest season, and the defenseless farmers couldn't afford to lose their grape crops, so they reluctantly allowed the militants to move into their mud-hut communities.

To oust the Taliban from the area, a joint force of American and Afghan troops launched Operation Kaika. As part of that action, Captain Sheffield Ford III spearheaded a unit of eight fellow Green Berets from Second Battalion, Seventh Special Forces Group, along with eight other American soldiers and 48 Afghan troops. Their mission: Clear out the Taliban from a village about 12 miles southwest of the city of Kandahar.

On a blistering hot day, June 23, 2006, Ford led the charge as his 65-man force stormed an enemy compound on the edge of the village. After engaging several militants in close combat, Ford and his troops secured the structure and turned it into their own patrol base. Then they set up a defensive perimeter.

What they didn't know was that hiding out in nearby villages were several hundred more insurgents, including a senior Taliban commander, all armed to the teeth with heavy weapons and sophisticated communications. Ford and his men were about to face the most daunting challenge of their lives — fighting for two days, nearly down to their last bullets, against a vastly larger force that repeatedly surrounded them.

As the sun sank behind the mountain peaks, the Taliban ignited a ferocious attack on the patrol base with a salvo of mortars that were blowing up inside the perimeter. Then the enemy began a full-out assault. Within minutes, they had completely encircled Ford's troops and were firing at them from all directions with small arms, machine guns, and RPGs.

Under withering fire, Ford jumped into the exposed turret of his Humvee and began shooting an M2 machine gun at the attackers. He paid little heed to the bullets and grenade fragments slamming into the sides of the vehicle. After a fellow Green Beret took over the weapon, Ford hustled to the rear of the Humvee to coordinate the defense of the patrol base, direct close air support, and maintain communication with headquarters back in Kandahar. While doing all that, he was forced to man the M240B machine gun because the Taliban assaults had intensified.

He knew that his men were battling a well-armed, determined enemy that far outnumbered them. As the conflict deepened, more militants entered the fray, convinced they had Ford and his men cornered. They began yelling and cursing at the Americans, taunting them with, "We're going to capture you!" and "You can't escape!" The enemy also shouted to the Afghan soldiers, "Give up and leave! We want only the Americans!"

The Taliban fighters' increasing firepower created enough fear in some of the Afghan defenders that they lost their confidence and hid behind walls rather than continue shooting. The Americans were having problems communicating with the Afghans because most of them didn't speak English. Completely exposed to enemy rounds and without concern for his own safety, Ford raced to the Afghan positions and, in rousing words relayed by an interpreter, convinced them to rejoin the fight. "We will never give up, and we will never back down!" he vowed.

At one point, insurgents broke through the perimeter, forcing Ford to call in close air support, even though there was a risk that an errant bomb could kill him and his men. Soon, the bombs and firepower from the aircraft overhead drove the militants back beyond the perimeter, but the aircrafts' muscle couldn't stop the Taliban from swarming around the patrol base. They were everywhere.

Realizing that his men needed help, Ford radioed ANP for backup. A responding force rushed toward the scene only to be ambushed by insurgents outside the village. The ANP never made it to the patrol base to help out. Ford and his men were on their own.

Although he and his troops were surrounded, the 34-year-old captain refused to get rattled. He had been in the army since he was 17, became a Special Forces enlisted man, and fought many bruising battles. But he had never experienced anything like this.

Ford refused to have his men simply hunker down and hold their perimeter. Instead, he chose to go on the offensive. Coordinating a bold counterattack, Ford led his troops in a push to regain the initiative. They shoved the insurgents back, forcing the enemy to withdraw and regroup. Fortunately, none of Ford's men was injured in the two-hour firefight.

Later, the Green Berets launched a small, remote-controlled airplane equipped with a video camera and flew it over the village. Near the town graveyard, about three-quarters of a mile from the patrol base, stood a structure labeled Compound 15. From the video transmitted by the plane, it was apparent that the militants were using the compound as their command center.

Master Sergeant Thom Maholic, the Special Forces team sergeant, volunteered to lead a patrol to knock out the command center. He was one of Ford's "fire-and-forget" guys—a term for extra-reliable soldiers who know how to get things done without any supervision. (The phrase is adapted from the military term for a missile that doesn't require further guidance after it is fired.)

For the mission, Maholic picked three other Americans, three Afghan interpreters, and 20 ANA soldiers. He split his patrol into two teams. The first team included Maholic, Sergeant First

Class Abram Hernandez, two interpreters, and 16 Afghan soldiers. Making up the second team were Staff Sergeant Matthew Binney; Staff Sergeant Joseph Fuerst III, a Florida National Guard infantryman attached to the Special Forces unit; an Afghan interpreter named Jacob; and four Afghan soldiers. The plan called for Maholic's team to assault Compound 15 after Binney and his men set up a machine gun 75 yards from the compound to provide cover fire for the attack team. They moved out before dawn.

At sunrise on a day when the temperature would reach 120 degrees, the patrol base was attacked again in another ferocious raid. Like before and without hesitation, Ford fired an M240B machine gun from an exposed position. As he continued shooting his weapon, he relayed instructions over the radio to organize the defense of the patrol base, coordinated the movements of Maholic's and Binney's teams, directed close air support, and updated headquarters. Overhead, helicopter gunships, A-10 Warthogs, and fighter jets pounded the enemy.

While the patrol base was under siege, Maholic prepared to assault Compound 15 when both his and Binney's teams were met with heavy resistance from concealed enemy positions near the command center. Binney and his men fought their way to their designated spot and set up their weapons by a vineyard within sight of Compound 15.

The vineyard had a series of three-foot-high mud walls parallel to one another with small ditches on either side. The top of each wall was hollowed out and filled with dirt that held wooden, trellislike stakes upon which the grapes grew. The walls, separated from one another by five-foot-wide aisles or lanes, had breaks in them about every 100 feet so farmers could move more freely through the vineyard.

After blasting their way past enemy positions, Maholic and his men attacked Compound 15 with fury. Wiping out the insurgents who were guarding the command center, the team charged into the compound and swiftly cleared the place of the remaining militants inside.

As Maholic was organizing his men into defensive positions, an unexpectedly large Taliban force of about 50 counterattacked, effectively surrounding and isolating his team. From various positions as close as 15 yards from the outside walls, the insurgents battered the compound with an uninterrupted barrage of machine gun, RPG, and small-arms fire. Maholic learned from intercepted radio transmissions that the enemy commander had ordered the Taliban fighters to capture the Americans alive.

From their vantage point by the vineyard, Binney and his men killed several militants, blunting the enemy's first attempt to retake the compound. But then the insurgents laced Binney's group with heavy fire from three machine guns. Forging ahead anyway, Binney and his men maneuvered their way to destroy a machine gun that had been raking the compound's walls.

While still on the move, Binney, Fuerst, and Jacob leaped through an opening in one of the vineyard's low mud walls and unknowingly stumbled into a pack of Taliban fighters. For a split second, both groups froze in surprise. But the trio reacted first with bursts of fire and hand grenades at close range, killing the enemy.

The three joined the rest of their small team just as another wave of enemy fighters swept within 15 yards of them. Uttering threats and insults at the Afghan soldiers, the militants closed in on Binney and his men.

To prevent being overrun, Binney jumped out from behind a wall to hurl a grenade at a nearby Taliban squad. But an enemy bullet struck a glancing blow in the back of his head and knocked him to the ground. The round hit with such force that it fractured his skull, causing him to temporarily lose his vision and hearing. When his hearing returned, it was accompanied by the loudest buzzing he had ever experienced. His vision came back, too, but it was blurry for several hours.

Struggling to regain his bearings and clear his head, Binney groped for his weapon and crawled back behind the wall. Even though his head was throbbing and bleeding, he refused medical attention and rejoined the battle, which by now was getting so intense that several Afghan soldiers panicked and tried to return to the patrol base. But they changed their minds after Binney persuaded them to fight. With renewed vigor, they fended off repeated assaults by the tenacious militants.

Suddenly, Fuerst crumpled in a heap from an RPG that struck and mangled his lower left leg but did not explode. When insurgents crept in on Fuerst, who was bleeding and sprawled out in the open, Binney led his team on a counterattack. Using hand grenades and small-arms fire, the soldiers tried to push the enemy back far enough so they could retrieve Fuerst.

Risking his own life, Binney jumped from behind his cover and ran toward his fallen buddy. Caught in the open, Binney was hit again, this time by a burst of machine-gun fire that destroyed his M4 carbine and shattered his left shoulder and upper arm. Binney maintained his composure as he lay wounded in pain.

Fuerst had a makeshift tourniquet around his knee, but it wasn't stopping the blood flow. Leaning against a small wall in the vineyard, he continued to shout out encouragement to the Afghan members of his team and directed their fire when they came under an even heavier fusillade from machine guns and RPGs.

Slumped by another wall, Binney passed his radio to Jacob, who called Captain Ford, pleading for a QRF to save them.

Four insurgents managed to get within shouting distance of the two wounded Americans and started taunting Jacob, a 23-year-old Afghan who had been translating for the Americans for three years. When he refused to respond to the verbal abuse, the militants changed their tone and said, "Hey, you're a fellow Muslim. We can forgive you. Just put your weapon down and walk away. We want the Americans alive."

Jacob replied, "Okay, come on over and get them."

The insurgents stopped firing and moved in on Binney and Fuerst, who by now were both fading in and out of consciousness. Jacob, meanwhile, sneaked over two aisles in the vineyard and then ambushed the militants, killing them one by one.

But then more Taliban fighters flocked into the vineyard. Jacob panicked and radioed Ford, "We're surrounded, and Binney and Fuerst are both wounded and in bad shape! There's no way out! The Taliban will take us hostage and torture us unless . . ." He paused, because what he was about to say next, out of desperation, made his stomach turn. "Unless I kill Fuerst and Binney and then myself, so that none of us will be taken alive."

"Absolutely not, Jacob!" bellowed Ford. "Help is on the way."

As long as Ford was in charge, he asserted, there was no way an American or Afghan soldier would be taken dead or alive by the Taliban.

In a flash, Sergeant First Class Brendan O'Connor, the team's senior medic, formed a ten-man rescue team that began fighting its way toward the vineyard where Binney and Fuerst lay wounded.

For the previous 40 minutes, Maholic had been sprinting across rooftops, climbing ladders, and ducking behind mud walls, adjusting his team's perimeter to keep the enemy from breaching Compound 15. When the defense began to falter because some of the Afghan soldiers were getting flustered and frightened, he dashed from one position to the next to rally them. "Show some guts!" he challenged them. "Engage the Taliban!"

He repositioned some of his men, identified enemy targets, directed fire, and shouted encouragement while almost single-handedly killing and wounding Taliban fighters with his automatic weapon. His determination, resolve, and bravery fired up the Afghans as they methodically beat back repeated Taliban assaults.

In another section of Compound 15, Sergeant First Class Abram Hernandez scaled an 18-foot-high, unstable homemade ladder to the top of a wall in order to get a better shooting angle on the militants. From this vulnerable position, he shot at the enemy and ducked down from incoming machine-gun fire and RPG explosions. Because he repeatedly was exposing his upper body above the top of the wall, the Taliban fighters began concentrating their fire on him. Hernandez defiantly remained on the wobbly ladder. When he spotted a swarm of insurgents searching the vineyard for the two wounded Americans, he kept firing at them, keeping them at bay while defending the compound from the enemy below.

As if that weren't enough to deal with, other militants scrambled up to the roof of a two-story building next door, providing them with a vantage point to fire directly into the compound at the rear of Hernandez's perch. Now he was drawing fire from opposite directions. While enemy bullets ripped into the outside of the wall that he was using for cover, more bullets began striking against the inside of the wall close to his exposed back. But Hernandez refused to reposition himself. His two injured comrades needed him to continue firing at the Taliban fighters who were trying to capture them. And his team members needed him to continue firing at those trying to retake the compound. So he kept shifting his aim, shooting at Taliban fighters in the vineyard, firing below in front of him, and swiveling to shoot at the ones behind him.

Soon O'Connor's rescue team made it to a wall near the vineyard. To reach the two wounded men, they would have to cross a 75-yard-wide grass field in a kill zone bordered by three enemy machine guns. O'Connor ordered his men to stay behind and cover him. Then, to his comrades' amazement, he shed his body armor so he could keep low to the ground and carry more medical supplies. He dropped into a shallow ditch and began crawling across the field as bullets zipped inches over him.

From his vantage point on the rickety ladder, Hernandez saw O'Connor's courageous crawl and fired at the enemy positions,

105

hoping to give his comrade some cover. But accurate enemy fire from behind Hernandez began to weaken the ladder. A machine-gun burst shredded the top part of the ladder and one of its legs, causing Hernandez to lose his balance as it collapsed to one side. He held on to the rung to keep from falling and then steadied himself by propping one leg against a corner of the wall.

Despite the bullets and RPG blasts, he refused to climb down, especially after seeing that a small Taliban squad was now making an all-out effort to hunt down O'Connor, who had made it to the vineyard. With one hand hanging on to the disintegrating ladder and the other firing his weapon, Hernandez began picking off the members of the enemy squad. His sharpshooting skills helped O'Connor reach Binney, Fuerst, and Jacob.

Maholic heard on his headset that O'Connor and the wounded were under heavy Taliban fire, so he ordered Hernandez to rush to their aid. That meant Maholic was the only American left to defend the compound with the Afghan soldiers.

Hernandez slipped out of the compound, maneuvered 200 yards—the length of two football fields—through Taliban fighting positions while dodging heavy fire and linked up with O'Connor. The two were working on a plan to get the wounded out of the vineyard when Hernandez received horrible news over his headset: Maholic had been shot.

Hernandez, who had been a medic before training as a Special Forces engineer, headed back toward the compound, crossing the same 200 yards he had just passed through, again while under intense direct fire from Taliban fighters. He bounded from one covered position to the next before sprinting the last few yards through machine-gun fire to reach the compound. Once inside, he raced to Maholic, who was slumped on the ground uncon-scious from a mortal wound. There was nothing Hernandez could do for his team sergeant but cradle him in his arms and watch him take his final breath.

An interpreter who saw the Green Beret fall told Hernandez that militants had closed within a few yards of the front gate and were ready to breach it, but Maholic was able to turn them back with his carbine. While spotting an insurgent sneaking in an alley, Maholic emerged from behind cover to shoot his weapon when he was hit by enemy fire.

Meanwhile, the rest of the rescue team hooked up with O'Connor and the two wounded soldiers in the vineyard. With gunships overhead providing suppressive fire, they headed for Compound 15. But by now Fuerst had died. He was the day's second KIA — killed in action.

At the patrol base, the other Americans were still fighting for their lives. When they learned of the deaths, some began to wonder if they, too, would end up as KIAs. They had been fighting for two days, had lost two men with another seriously wounded, and were almost out of ammunition, water, and food.

During a brief lull in the battle, several soldiers jotted quick notes and put them in their pockets, thinking that if they should die, their letters might be read by their loved ones. Grieving over the loss of his buddies, Staff Sergeant Brandon Pechette pulled out a little notebook and penned a short note to his wife. He told her that he and his comrades were surrounded, outnumbered, and were running out of supplies. But he ended the letter in a defiant tone: "If I'm going to die, I'm taking as many Taliban as I can with me. We're all going to fight as bravely as we can."

And so they did. With the help of continuous vital air support, Ford and his men successfully withstood what had been an almost overwhelming series of assaults.

Back at Compound 15, O'Connor rallied the troops who were demoralized by Maholic's death. The medical sergeant directed the evacuation of Binney and the bodies of Maholic and Fuerst. He also arranged for the resupply of food, water, and ammunition for the troops in the compound. Then, after dark settled in, he led them safely back to the patrol base, which was no longer under attack.

While they still had effective air support, Ford ordered everyone to pack up. They hopped into their vehicles and headed home to Firebase Gecko in Kandahar. After 17½ hours of intense combat over two days in unbearable heat against a much larger foe, the Green Berets and their Afghan comrades had killed more than 125 Taliban fighters while losing two Americans and three Afghan interpreters. It had been one of the largest battles in Afghanistan since the American invasion in 2001.

At an emotional ceremony in Kandahar, the Green Berets honored the two courageous fallen warriors, Thom Maholic and Joe Fuerst.

As a Florida National Guardsman, Fuerst, 26, was a police academy graduate preparing for a law-enforcement career. He and his wife, Tara, had bought an acre of land in Brooksville, Florida, where they had planned to build a house and start a family. Tara was also deployed to Afghanistan as a member of her husband's National Guard unit, Fifty-third Infantry Brigade.

Maholic, 38, who loved NASCAR and music, was born and raised in Pennsylvania. He had married his childhood sweetheart,

Wendy, and was the father of a son. The team sergeant was so respected by his fellow Green Berets that Firebase Gecko was renamed in his honor. It is now called Firebase Maholic.

Sheffield Ford's team became the most decorated Special Forces unit for a single battle in Afghanistan.

Ford, who was promoted to major, was awarded the Silver Star for his steadfast bravery and combat skills in the face of tremendous odds. "Ford's courageous actions and determined leadership in the face of an overwhelming attack by a well-armed and determined enemy force prevented the destruction of his encircled detachment," reads the narrative accompanying the award. It also cites "his gallantry, dedication to duty, and selfless sacrifice."

Also receiving Silver Stars were Staff Sergeant Matthew Binney, who survived his serious injuries, and Sergeant First Class Abram Hernandez. Master Sergeant Thom Maholic was posthumously awarded the same medal.

Awarded Bronze Stars with Valor were Staff Sergeant Charles Lyles, Staff Sergeant Michael Sanabria, and Sergeant First Class Ebbon Brown of Seventh Special Forces Group. Staff Sergeant Joseph Fuerst was awarded the Bronze Star posthumously.

Honored with the Distinguished Service Cross — the military's second-highest medal for combat valor — was Sergeant First Class Brendan O'Connor, whose gripping story of courage during this battle is presented in the next chapter.

The Crawl for Life

SERGEANT FIRST CLASS
BRENDAN O'CONNOR

Under a barrage of bullets and RPG blasts, Sergeant First Class Brendan O'Connor crouched behind a mud wall and sized up the dire situation: Two of his buddies were seriously injured and hiding about 75 yards away in a vineyard infested with Taliban fighters bent on capturing them.

The only way for him to reach the dying men would be to low-crawl along a 16-inch-deep ditch across two-thirds of a grass field in a kill zone covered by three enemy machine guns. Then he would have to jump up and run the last 25 yards for his life . . . and his buddies.

During his extensive training, the senior Special Forces medic had been taught to let the wounded come to him or let others bring them to him, because his skills were too valuable to the rest of his team to risk his injury or death. But now there were two fellow soldiers who would surely die without his help. *No one can reach them, and they can't come to me*, he thought. *I can't just sit and wait for this battle to end. Those two guys don't stand a chance unless I go to them now.*

Contrary to what he had been taught, he went after them. He began slithering forward on his stomach as the Taliban machine gunners zeroed in on him. Even though bullets mowed the grass inches above his head, he kept edging forward. But his body armor was acting like a plow, gathering dirt in front of him and raising his profile. He stopped. *I can't get low enough to the ground. I have to turn around.* He crawled back to the wall and once again did something that was totally against everything he had learned during his training. He removed the only protection he had from enemy fire — his Interceptor bulletproof vest. Then he slid back into the shallow ditch and began his perilous crawl through the kill zone without any body armor at all. *Here's hoping I can stay low enough.*

O'Connor was one of nine Green Berets from Second Battalion, Seventh Special Forces Group, who, along with eight other American soldiers and forty-eight Afghan troops, went on a mission to clear the Taliban from a village near Kandahar.

At age 45, O'Connor was by far the oldest American in the unit, prompting some of his comrades to jokingly call him "Old Blue" after the elderly, gray-haired character Joseph "Blue" Palasky in the movie comedy *Old School*. But when it came to combat and saving lives, O'Connor's age meant nothing. He was the one everyone counted on.

Born at the U.S. Military Academy at West Point, O'Connor

came from a distinguished family of servicemen. His father, Lieutenant Colonel Mort O'Connor, a West Point graduate, was a true "warrior-poet." He taught English literature at the academy and was also decorated several times for valor on the battlefield. Tragically, in 1968 when Brendan was seven years old, his father was killed in action in Vietnam while leading men into combat as commander of First Infantry Division's First Battalion, Second Infantry.

Brendan O'Connor's grandfather (Mort O'Connor's father) was Brigadier General Bill O'Connor, who served in Europe during World War II, including at the Battle of the Bulge. The general and three of his brothers (Brendan's great-uncles) were all West Pointers.

So it was only natural that Brendan would seek a career in the military. For 15 years, he served as a Special Forces officer in the Army Reserves. Then he had a calling to pursue medicine, so he took the uncommon step of giving up his commission. In 1994, he enlisted in the army to become a Special Forces medical sergeant. After rigorous training, he was deployed to more than a dozen hot spots throughout the world before being sent to Afghanistan.

On June 23, 2006, O'Connor and his comrades, led by Captain Sheffield Ford III, stormed an enemy compound on the edge of the village and turned it into their own patrol base, which they repeatedly had to defend against a much larger Taliban force.

The next morning, Master Sergeant Thom Maholic, the Special Forces team sergeant; Sergeant First Class Abram Hernandez; three interpreters and sixteen Afghan soldiers attacked and took over Compound 15, the Taliban's command center, about three-quarters of a mile away. A second team of Staff Sergeant Matthew Binney; Staff Sergeant Joseph F. Fuerst III, a Florida National Guard infantryman; an interpreter named Jacob; and four Afghan soldiers provided cover fire from a nearby vineyard.

At the same time, however, the militants struck the patrol base again in another fierce attempt to overpower the outnumbered troops. Doing his part to keep the enemy from breaching the perimeter, O'Connor was switching between his M4 carbine and a machine gun on an up-armored Humvee. Even though he was exposed in the turret, he braved the bullets and shrapnel that were hitting all around him. Sweat drenched his uniform as the temperature climbed to 120 degrees.

O'Connor was wearing a radio headset that monitored Maholic's and Binney's patrols, but he was so focused on firing his weapons that he wasn't listening to their transmissions to Ford. He didn't realize at first that Maholic and his men in Compound 15 were under siege from a Taliban counterattack. Nor did he hear that Binney and Fuerst were seriously wounded and that Jacob, the interpreter, feared they would be captured.

"Get over here quick," Ford radioed O'Connor from another section of the patrol base. "We need to get some help out to one of the patrols."

O'Connor rushed over to Ford, who told him about Binney and Fuerst.

"Well, I better go out there and get them," O'Connor said.

Talking over the radio in a voice shaking with fear, Jacob told O'Connor, "Matthew's been hit in the head and shoulder, and Joe's unconscious and his leg is bleeding. We're surrounded, and you need to get over here as fast as you can!"

"Where are you?"

"I don't know exactly. Somewhere in the vineyard southwest of the compound."

"Hang on, Jacob. We're on our way."

O'Connor stuffed his pockets and pouches with bandages, IVs, tourniquets, and other medical supplies. Then he formed a rescue team that included Sergeant First Class Sean Mishra, an Oregon National Guardsman; an Afghan interpreter; and seven ANA soldiers. He and his men broke out of their perimeter and fought their way to a knoll in the center of the graveyard where they could see Maholic running from one end of Compound 15 to the other, firing at the enemy while coordinating the defense.

They also could see Hernandez balanced on a tall shaky ladder, which was beginning to teeter at an awkward angle against a wall. He was directing fire toward a group of insurgents in the nearby vineyard. *That's probably where Matthew, Joe, and Jacob are pinned down*, O'Connor thought. Watching tracer rounds pelt the wall next to Hernandez, the medic told himself, *I'm amazed he's still propped on that ladder, firing away. That's absolutely inspiring.*

When O'Connor and his men ran across the cemetery, they received enemy fire from the south. But they made it to Compound 15, where Maholic pointed out Binney and Fuerst's general location in the vineyard. "They won't last much longer without your help," Maholic said. "Hernandez is doing his best to lay down suppressive fire."

The rescue team left the compound and moved along a wall while taking fire from machine guns and RPGs. The group sneaked behind a slight rise in the ground that concealed its movement.

The change in elevation petered out, leading to a 16-inch-deep irrigation ditch that cut across two-thirds of an open 75-yard-wide grass field. On the other side was the vineyard. But off to the right, the Taliban had three machine guns trained on the kill zone.

Turning to Mishra, O'Connor said, "Sean, you and the others set up a machine gun and give me some cover fire."

"What are you going to do?"

"I'm going to crawl in the ditch across the field."

"But the ditch doesn't go all the way."

"I know. At the end of the ditch, I'll dash for the vineyard. If I time it right with your suppressive fire, you'll keep the enemy's machine gunners down, and I'll be okay."

With his 9-mm pistol attached to his chest, O'Connor started to low-crawl on his stomach, but the going was agonizingly slow. Because he was carrying medical supplies, grenade pouches, ammo pouches, communications gear, and body armor, his back was protruding over the top of the ditch by about six inches, making him an easy target.

That wasn't his only problem. As he squirmed forward on his stomach, his body armor was digging into the dirt and acting like a plow. *This isn't going to work*, he thought. *I can't get low enough with all this equipment and my body armor.* Reluctantly, he turned back.

"How are you going to get to Matthew and Joe?" Mishra asked.

"I'll show you." O'Connor slipped out of his body armor and stripped off his battle gear, which together weighed close to 80 pounds. Then he stuffed his pockets with ammo and medical supplies.

"You're going back out there without body armor?" Mishra asked.

"It's the only way. I need the mobility."

O'Connor pulled out a ground-to-air identity marker and tucked the two-by-two-foot bright orange silky fabric under his back collar. He wanted to alert the pilots of the gunships above that he was a friendly.

"Sean, you and the others stay here until I get to the vineyard. I'll recon the area first to look for the enemy and find our guys. I'll want your help later when we try to get them out of there."

Once again, O'Connor got down on his stomach and began the challenging low crawl across the field. The militants detected his movement and trained their machine guns at him. An eruption of bullets skimmed over the top of the ditch, cutting the grass and, in some places, actually setting the blades on fire. Inch by inch, O'Connor worked his way along the ditch.

He looked back once and saw an Afghan soldier next to a wall shooting at the Taliban machine gunners who were trying to kill the medic. The gunners turned their fire toward the soldier, who clumsily leaped behind the wall just as the rounds disintegrated part of it. The Afghan was unhurt. Seeing the soldier's arms and legs flail in the air during his dive for cover, O'Connor couldn't help but laugh. For just a few seconds, the comical sight had taken the medic's mind off the grim danger he was facing.

When the ditch began leveling off with the grass, O'Connor stopped crawling. He still had another 25 yards to go, but this he would have to do standing up. He waited for Mishra and the

Afghan soldiers to lay down suppressive fire before he sprang to his feet and sprinted the rest of the way to the vineyard.

Now that O'Connor had made it safely across the field, he engaged in a deadly game of hide-and-seek — hide from the enemy and seek the wounded. Cautiously, he crept into the web of tangled grapevines. "Jacob?" he called out in a loud whisper.

"Over here," Jacob replied in a hushed tone.

O'Connor hopped over one of the vineyard's low walls and walked toward the voice. "Jacob?" he softly said again. This time there was no response. *The enemy must be so close that he's afraid to respond. He doesn't want to give away his exact location, but I think I know where he is.*

Stepping around the bodies of several dead fighters whom Jacob and Hernandez had killed, O'Connor crept closer to the interpreter and the wounded. Then he heard footsteps on the other side of the wall. *Taliban!* They were just beyond where he thought Jacob was, so O'Connor detoured around them.

He found Jacob sitting upright and pressed against a mud wall. The interpreter put his fingers to his mouth in a signal to remain quiet, then pointed to the wall on the left, indicating the enemy was on the other side.

Once the enemy fighters moved on, O'Connor scrambled over to Fuerst a few yards away. Fuerst was ashen and unconscious, his lower left leg nearly torn off by the unexploded RPG warhead that lay next to him. He had lost a lot of blood from the massive blunt trauma, even though a handkerchief had been tied over Fuerst's left knee as a makeshift tourniquet. But the tourniquet was ineffective and had allowed blood to flow for the last 40 minutes. The medic checked his vital signs. They indicated Fuerst was close to death. O'Connor applied a new tourniquet and tried to get Fuerst to respond.

But then Taliban forces got a bead on the Americans' position, forcing O'Connor and Jacob to duck from enemy fire and RPG blasts. As the two shot back, gunships overhead were busy holding back the militants.

While working on Fuerst, O'Connor called out to Binney, who was slouched in shock and pain on the other side of the opposite wall.

"Matt, what's going on, man?" O'Connor said.

"Oh," Binney groaned. Gasping between words, he mumbled, "I'm hit . . . in the head . . . and in my arm . . . and my head . . . really hurts."

"You'll have to move to me because I have to take care of Joe. He can't help himself."

Binney, who was also a medic, rasped, "I'm so weak . . . body is shutting down . . . lost feeling in legs . . . losing too much blood."

"Matt, you have to push yourself over to me. You can do it."

Hearing O'Connor's supportive voice, Binney dug his heels in the dirt and, with his back pressed against the wall, tried to stand up. Just as he started to slump over, he was caught by an Afghan soldier, who had made it to the vineyard. With the soldier's help, Binney got over the wall where it was slightly safer.

O'Connor began treating Binney, then went back and forth between him and Fuerst. The medic was worried that Binney had internal bleeding because one of the bullets had pierced his shoulder and exited his armpit, pulverizing the humerus — the upper bone that connects the shoulder with the elbow — near a major blood vessel. *Any sudden movement of those bones and joints could cause a tear or rupture of the vessel*, O'Connor thought. He put on a splint to stabilize the break and bandaged the arm to Binney's body to keep it from moving.

Several times while he was treating the wounded, O'Connor was forced to put down his medical supplies and pick up his weapon to keep the Taliban fighters from overrunning his position. He reported his situation to the rest of his team members, who were still pinned down on the other side of the field.

"We can't stay here much longer if Joe has any chance at surviving," O'Connor radioed Ford, who was busy directing the defense of the patrol base from repeated attacks. Hearing that O'Connor, Jacob, and the wounded men needed help, Maholic sent Hernandez, who ran 200 yards past enemy positions to reach them.

While working on a plan to get the wounded out of the vineyard, Hernandez received news over his headset that made him grimace. "Thom's been hit and it's bad," Hernandez told O'Connor. "I have to go back right now. You'll need to get Joe and Matt out of here on your own."

O'Connor figured it was too dangerous to move the wounded back across the field. He radioed his team to meet him at a nearby orchard house east of the vineyards. The medic tied Fuerst's legs together and then, with Jacob's help, lifted his unconscious comrade over his shoulder. With Binney leaning on the Afghan soldier, the group headed out.

Dodging enemy fire and RPGs, O'Connor carried Fuerst for about 200 yards and over two walls in plain view of the enemy until they reached a lane where Mishra and the rest of the Afghans helped them over another wall that was six feet high. They all found cover behind the orchard house.

While it was getting pounded by enemy fire, O'Connor tried to revive Fuerst, who was barely clinging to life. The medic elevated the victim's leg so the flow of blood went toward the heart and lungs, causing Fuerst to let out a moan. O'Connor pleaded, "Stay with me, Joe! Stay with me!" The medic pulled out an IV set from his medical bag, but the sweltering heat had melted the glue that kept the set together. O'Connor refused to give up on Fuerst and continued working on him and Binney with his limited medical supplies.

Then, after putting Fuerst on a foldable litter and assisting Binney, the group hustled over the same open field that O'Connor had crossed earlier. But this time they had gunships overhead that provided the necessary suppressive fire. As they neared Compound 15, Fuerst went into cardiac arrest, so O'Connor stopped to perform CPR on him. The medic worked feverishly, but Fuerst was too far gone to be revived.

When the team reached the compound, O'Connor was hoping that even though one life had been lost, he could save another. He rushed over to Hernandez and said, "Let me see if I can help Thom."

Hernandez shook his head and, in a voice choking with emotion, said, "It's no use. He took a bullet in the head. When I reached him, he was unresponsive and there was nothing I could do. He died in my arms."

Shoving aside his grief, O'Connor took charge of the compound's defense in order to keep him and the rest of the troops from being captured. The defense was shaky because morale had sunk among the disheartened men. Their inspiring team leader Maholic was dead. And so were Fuerst and three interpreters. Many of the Afghan soldiers were holing up in the compound, just hoping they could survive. That seemed like a long shot, considering they were running out of ammo, water, and food. O'Connor personally knew many of the Afghans, because they had trained with the Green Berets and successfully carried out several missions without a single injury.

"We have to rise to the challenge, or they'll be carrying all of us out of here in body bags," he told the troops. With Hernandez's help, he repositioned the men to shore up spots in the defense that were most vulnerable to attack. Strengthened by a newfound spirit, the Afghan soldiers rallied and put up such a hard-hitting resistance that the enemy withdrew, although the compound was still surrounded. Some of the troops were almost down to their last bullet, forcing Hernandez to scrounge up rounds from the wounded and dead.

O'Connor believed his team couldn't fight their way back to the patrol base while carrying two bodies and an injured soldier. He examined Binney. *Matthew can't make it that far. He's hanging on, but he's in a lot of pain. We need to medevac him out, and we need to get supplies in.*

He radioed for an Air Force Special Operations combat helicopter whose crew was willing to set down in an unsecured landing zone. "Those guys will do anything to help," he told Hernandez. "They're ready to fight their way in and out."

With the assistance of other attack aircraft in the area, O'Connor and his men pushed the militants back far enough so that the helicopter could land. The crew dropped off the needed supplies and picked up the casualties.

O'Connor hadn't eaten for nearly a day and barely had time to consume anything but water. It didn't matter, because he was running on adrenaline.

Apache gunships continued to hammer Taliban positions into the night. Finally it was decided to evacuate the compound and return to the patrol base with the supplies. An AC-130 gunship marked a direct path with an infrared beam that could be seen only through NVGs. The pilots of the Apaches and air force gunships were ordered to attack anyone seen moving outside the path. Donning his NVGs, O'Connor followed the beam and, undetected by the enemy, led the men safely back to the patrol base, which was no longer under attack. The Taliban had given up. They had been badly beaten.

As the troops' convoy headed back to their firebase in Kandahar, O'Connor tried to unwind. He was tired, hungry, and achy after two tense days of dodging bullets, shooting militants, and rallying Afghans; of running through kill zones, crawling in ditches and climbing over walls; of reaching the wounded, treating the injuries, and carrying the dying.

When he finally reached the firebase, he paused in his Humvee, put his hands on his knees, and took several deep breaths. He could finally relax.

For his courageous actions during the two-day battle in 2006, Brendan O'Connor, who was promoted to master sergeant, was awarded the Distinguished Service Cross, the military's second-highest medal for valor. It was only the second time that the award had been given to a soldier who served in Afghanistan. He was also named Army Special Operations Command Medic of the Year.

"For the men who were with him that day, Master Sergeant O'Connor is a savior," said Admiral Eric T. Olson, commander of United States Special Operations Command, who presented the Distinguished Service Cross to O'Connor at Fort Bragg, North Carolina, on April 30, 2008. "For all Americans, he is a hero, and for all members of special operations across the services, he is a source of enormous pride."

Upon receiving the medal in front of his fellow Green Berets, his wife, Margaret, and his four children, O'Connor said, "I've never been more honored, but this medal belongs to my whole team. Every member was watching out for the other, inspiring each other, and for some, sacrificing for each other. We all fought hard, and it could just as easily be any one of them standing up here getting this medal. Every one of them is a hero."

O'Connor was awarded the Distinguished Service Cross almost 40 years to the day after his father was killed in combat in Vietnam.

Death Struggle

STAFF SERGEANT JASON FETTY

Staff Sergeant Jason Fetty stared into the crazed eyes of a suicide bomber and thought, *I'm not going to let him kill innocent people.*

Men, women, children, government officials, and dignitaries had gathered on the grounds of the local hospital to celebrate the opening of a much-needed emergency room built with the help of the U.S. military.

The bomb-laden terrorist was determined to twist this feel-good ceremony into a bloody scene of death and destruction.

Fetty was just as determined to stop him.

But the two were locked in a deadly tug-of-war. Fetty was clutching his rifle while the terrorist was yanking on the weapon's barrel. The soldier didn't dare shoot during this nerve-wracking struggle, because too many civilians stood in harm's way. And

Fetty couldn't take him down on the spot without risking an explosion that potentially could kill dozens in the crowd, including the governor.

I have to do something before we all blow up.

Jason Fetty was about as far away as he could be from his hometown of Parkersburg, West Virginia, where he was known as a caring pharmacist and a dedicated Army Reserve soldier. When he was called up for active duty in Afghanistan, it came as no surprise to family and friends that the 32-year-old citizen-soldier volunteered to join a unit tasked with winning the hearts and minds of the Afghan people.

He was a member of a Provisional Reconstruction Team, or PRT. Each of the more than two dozen PRTs in Afghanistan consists of a group of about 100 people from the United States and other countries, including military personnel, officials from government agencies, diplomats, advisors, and civilian experts. Their job is to help build up a war-weary country plagued by hardship, suicide bombings, insurgent attacks, and a weak government. Over the years, PRTs have improved roads, bridges, and dams; built or repaired schools, medical facilities, and municipal buildings; drilled wells; increased security; trained local police, government officials, and farmers; and worked with tribal leaders and mullahs to find ways of meeting the basic needs of the people.

In Fetty's mind, offering a helping hand was as effective — if not more so — as firing a weapon in defeating the insurgency and winning the peace. It was still dangerous work. PRTs have always been a threat to the enemy because these units offer hope, opportunity, and a promise of a better life for the Afghan people.

As a member of 364th Civil Affairs Brigade, Fetty served in a PRT in Khost Province. His base was just miles from the former home of the al-Qaeda camps that trained the terrorists who carried out the 9/11 attacks.

When Fetty arrived, the people in the region were dealing with dangerous unpaved mountain roads, virtually no electrical power or sanitation, and few schools or health-care facilities in rural areas. Adding to their misery, al-Qaeda, Taliban, and other fundamentalist fighters were spreading extremist views and terror.

Every day during his tour of duty, Fetty was reminded of the ruthlessness of the Taliban and their severe interpretation of Islamic rule. Afghans told him of being punished for reading books, of women being beaten and tortured for attending school. The father of one of his interpreters was killed by the Taliban solely because he was a physician who believed in Western medicine. Another interpreter was thrown in prison because he had the nerve to trim his facial hair.

Fetty saw firsthand how fanatical insurgents willingly blew themselves up in a demented effort to kill those who opposed them. Midway through his deployment, he was riding in an army convoy, returning from a mail run, when a suicide bomber jumped on the hood of one of the Humvees and detonated his explosive-filled vest. None of the soldiers was hurt, but the blast killed an innocent little girl who was standing on the side of the road. Her mangled body left several hardened soldiers reduced to tears.

But for every heartbreak, he saw scores of big and little victories. One of the pet projects of Fetty's PRT was the construction of an emergency room at Khost City Hospital. As part of his duties, Fetty visited the site every other week to conduct quality checks throughout the building process. He became friendly with the doctors and nurses, who were thrilled that they would soon work in a real ER instead of the crowded, makeshift room that currently handled emergencies.

Finally, after months of hard work, the new building was completed. To celebrate this accomplishment, the PRT planned a ribbon-cutting ceremony for February 20, 2007. The public was invited along with tribal leaders, mullahs, local dignitaries, and government officials. The governor of the province, Arsalah Jamal, agreed to give a speech heralding the achievement. Fetty, who was only a few weeks from completing his tour of duty and going home, viewed the upcoming ceremony as a satisfying way to cap his 11 months in Afghanistan.

Despite rumors and spotty intelligence warning of a possible suicide attack at the event, the PRT refused to cancel the ceremony. Fetty knew that the terrorists were always trying to kill pro-American officials and destroy new projects that would benefit a community. Nevertheless, he agreed with the decision to go ahead with the event because its success would be another blow against the insurgents.

As one of the persons in charge of security for the ceremony, Fetty assumed Governor Jamal would be a likely assassin's target for aligning himself with the Americans. The city already had lost two sub-governors to suicide bombs within the previous months.

Fetty and his comrades had trained hard to prevent most every kind of attack at a public event, including those involving suicide bombers. *Fanatics are nearly impossible to stop,* he thought. *The likelihood of another attempt is pretty high.* When he arrived at the hospital grounds on the day of the event, he promised himself to do everything possible to make sure nothing bad would happen.

The hospital sat inside a walled compound. The ceremony was set up outside on one side of the compound so patients and medical staff could still enter and leave the building without having the crowd block their way. Although Fetty wanted as many locals as possible to attend the community event, he also needed to display a show of force. He set up an outer security perimeter of ANP and an inner one made up of PRT members and soldiers from Eighty-second Airborne Division who were on their first mission in Khost.

Armed with an M4 carbine, Fetty positioned himself in front of the hospital entrance. With a careful eye, he watched the people gather around a small podium 30 yards from him where the governor and chief of the hospital would soon speak. *It's a real nice crowd,* Fetty thought. *Must be close to two hundred people.* It was a scene that never would have taken place if American-led forces hadn't ousted the Taliban from power.

Spotting a boy in the crowd, Fetty strolled over and began making funny faces. The soldier liked to joke with young people so they would be less afraid of Americans. The boy and several nearby Afghans laughed at his antics.

Suddenly, Fetty heard a commotion coming from the hospital entrance. Doctors, nurses, and other medical personnel were streaming out the door and running by him, breaking through the inner security perimeter. He recognized the frightened faces of the hospital staffers. But he was worried that because the new soldiers didn't know the workers, the soldiers might use lethal force to stop them from breaching the perimeter. Fetty shouted, "Don't shoot!" The last thing he wanted was for an innocent person to get shot by an American soldier.

Something bad must be happening inside, he thought as more staff members fled the building. He wheeled around and saw a strange man walking out of the entrance toward him. The person was in no hurry. He looked around, as if getting his bearings, and then stared at the podium where the governor was chatting with local officials.

The first thing Fetty noticed was that the man — about five feet eight inches tall, stocky and bearded — was wearing a white doctor's coat. *I know most everyone in the hospital*, the soldier thought. *He's not one of them.* Then Fetty studied the man's eyes. They were wild and wide. *He looks crazed, like he's on drugs.* Fetty figured something wasn't right. He could feel it in his gut — a sinking feeling that things were about to go bad. Really bad.

Fetty's body tensed. He wasn't positive but he suspected the man had an explosive vest underneath his coat. *Suicide bomber!*

The man's dark eyes were darting back and forth as if scanning for the right place to blow himself up and take the most people with him. *He's looking for the shortest route to his target. He's planning to kill the governor and everyone around him. I have to stop him!*

The man stepped toward Fetty without saying a word, so the soldier began his "escalation of force" commands: "Stop! Get down!"

Ignoring the order, the man moved closer until he was within reach of the barrel of Fetty's weapon and tried to grab it.

Fetty backed up. His index finger was wrapped around the trigger of his M4, but he didn't squeeze it. He was afraid to give a warning shot because of the possibility that the bullet could ricochet and harm one or more of the persons standing only a few feet away from him. *I don't have the right angle to shoot him now. But if I keep backing up, he could try to rush me and take my weapon. I need to get him away from the crowd so I can get a better shot.*

The man continued to close in until he clutched the rifle barrel and pulled on it. Rather than shake him off, Fetty used the dangerous tug-of-war to his advantage. The five-foot eleven-inch, 180-pound soldier turned so that the attacker's back was to the ceremony. Slowly, Fetty moved him away from the crowd.

If he grabs hold of my armor or my uniform in any way, I'm toast. If I try to push him away, I won't be able to stop him from detonating himself. Fetty had to stay calm but forceful.

Ever so carefully, Fetty maneuvered him toward a clearing between the hospital and the nearby administrative huts, farther from the people who were starting to shove their way in the opposite direction once they realized what was happening.

Fetty kept his eyes locked on the terrorist's eyes. *I have to keep him focused on me and not his primary target. I can't let him kill the governor.* "Come on," he whispered to himself. "Keep your attention on me." *If I stall him long enough, everyone in the security team should be doing their job and getting the area cleared.*

Fetty figured that any of the soldiers who saw the confrontation knew better than to shoot for fear of hitting him or an innocent bystander. He was on his own — at least until the others had a better shooting angle.

As the two men continued to struggle over the weapon, Fetty thought, *I probably won't survive, because he's going to blow us up.* The soldier accepted that he probably was seconds away from sure death. He stopped thinking about his own survival. *It's better if I die only with the bomber than with the governor and thirty other people in the crowd.*

When he felt they were far enough away from the crowd, Fetty decided to go on the attack. *I either kill him or he kills me.* He took a deep breath, jerked the rifle barrel out of the man's grip and, in a continuing motion, flipped his weapon so he could slam the butt into the attacker's chin.

The terrorist staggered for a moment, so Fetty gave him a shoulder tackle that sent both of them sprawling to the ground. The soldier scrambled to his feet and fired a couple of rounds into the ground next to the man's sandals. "Stay down!" ordered Fetty, hoping the man wouldn't rise.

But the terrorist got up and rushed forward, so Fetty shot him in his shins and then his kneecap. The attacker crumbled to the ground. *That should keep him down.* But it didn't. To Fetty's dismay, the man staggered to his feet. *He must be so high on drugs that he can't even feel the pain.* The terrorist then charged him one more time. Fetty shot him again, this time in the lower stomach. Fetty didn't want to test his luck by shooting into the attacker's suicide vest, which increased the risk of blowing them up.

From about 20 yards away, Second Lieutenant Josh Phillips, Second Battalion, 231st Airborne Field Artillery Regiment, had been circling the two, waiting for a clear shot. After Fetty worked the terrorist toward a wall, Fetty stepped away. Seeing that it was safe to shoot, Phillips fired at the man twice.

When he first spotted Fetty in trouble, Navy Petty Officer First Class James Hamill, a command photographer who was there to take pictures of the ceremony, dropped his camera and raised his rifle. Closing in from the opposite side until he was only ten feet away, Hamill opened fire on the terrorist at the same time Phillips did, catching the attacker in a cross fire.

The man went down hard, wounded so severely there was no chance he could get back up. Lying on his stomach, he lifted his head and glared at Fetty with a look of hatred. The attacker had failed in his mission to kill the governor and dozens of innocent people. And it was all because of the soldier standing in front of him. The terrorist said nothing, but his fury-filled eyes made it clear that he now had only one target left worth dying for — Fetty.

I know what you're going to do next, thought Fetty.

With a quivering hand, the man reached under his coat. *He's going for his suicide vest! This is it. He's going to blow both of us up!*

Fetty spun around, took two giant steps, and then dived toward a small dirt embankment 15 yards away. Before he reached it, a deafening explosion shook the compound. For a fleeting moment, while Fetty was still in the air, he thought he was dead because the percussion was so powerful. He landed in a heap. Then everything went silent. The stunned soldier couldn't breathe for several seconds, because the force had knocked the wind out of him.

As the choking dust began to settle, Fetty realized he had fallen on top of his rifle. When he tried to sit up, he saw blood dripping on his weapon. He knew he was bleeding badly from his face, but he didn't feel anything at first because he was in shock. Then the pain began to spread across his head and down the left side of his body. The blast had peppered him from head to toe with shrapnel, ripping gashes in his face, back, elbow, torso, leg, and ankle. His jaw was cracked open, too.

Six other soldiers, including Phillips and Hamill, and an Afghan security guard were injured in the blast. Fortunately, no one in the crowd was hurt. When the bomb exploded, Phillips dived for cover but still sustained shrapnel wounds to his left hand. Hamill wasn't quite as lucky. A piece of shrapnel tore into his abdomen. Ignoring the pain, he performed first aid on some of the other injured soldiers who were worse off than him. He also helped ensure the area was secure in case of a follow-up attack before he agreed to get treated.

All that remained of the suicide bomber was a big hole in the ground.

An investigation of the attempted attack revealed that the terrorist, posing as a doctor, had slipped through the Afghan police's outer security perimeter. When he was questioned minutes later, his crazed behavior — apparently a result of the drugs he needed to carry out his deadly mission — triggered a panic among the hospital staff. That was when Fetty sprang into action.

Shortly after the foiled attempt, local leaders and mullahs staged a peace rally. They were upset that a terrorist tried to kill the governor and innocent people on the grounds of a hospital. They decreed such cowardly acts of violence "un-Islamic." They urged Afghans to spread the word that the U.S. military was there to help them, and that Americans — especially soldiers like Jason Fetty — were risking their lives to make the country a better place to live.

For his quick-thinking actions, Staff Sergeant Jason Fetty was awarded the Silver Star, becoming the first Army Reserve soldier to receive the medal for valor in Afghanistan. He also was given the Purple Heart for his wounds.

"His actions, along with the actions of others on the team, really prevented a strategic catastrophe," said Navy Commander John F. G. Wade, who headed the Joint Provisional Reconstruction Team in Khost. "He saved countless lives. It was an incredible honor to have served with him."

Navy Petty Officer First Class James Hamill was awarded the Bronze Star with Valor for his role in thwarting the suicide bomber. He also received the Purple Heart, as did Second Lieutenant Josh Phillips.

Saving
Private Moss

MAJOR JOHN OH

Major John Oh, a surgeon on duty at a small base in southeastern Afghanistan, was waiting for a medevac helicopter to land outside his makeshift field hospital. The crew had radioed him that among the four casualties on board from an ambush was a soldier in critical condition with severe shrapnel wounds to the abdomen. His blood pressure was dropping and his heart rate was dangerously high—definite signs that he was in shock and losing blood. In military medical terms, he was an "urgent surgical."

When the chopper arrived, the patient, who was covered in a blanket, was carried on a stretcher straight into the battle aid station (BAS). Oh noticed that the young man was completely pale, barely conscious, and cold. The surgeon and his medical team threw off the blanket and stripped off the patient's clothes so they could assess the wounds. Oh was cutting the bandages on the left side of the patient's hip when he saw something wrapped next to the pelvis that made him freeze. A metal rod with a tail fin was sticking out of the soldier's side.

Oh had never seen an RPG up close before, but he knew immediately that was what it was. "Unexploded round!" he yelled to his team. "Everybody get out!"

After Oh and his team hurried to put on helmets and body armor, he had only seconds to work out in his mind what to do next: *If we try to save him, we run the risk that the RPG could explode, killing us all. If we don't do something right away, he will bleed to death.*

On the morning of March 16, 2006, a platoon from Alpha Company, Second Battalion, Eighty-Seventh Infantry, Third Brigade Combat Team, Tenth Mountain Division, which had been in country barely a month, was on its first patrol. A convoy of five American Humvees and a pickup truck loaded with nine Afghan soldiers rumbled through a pass in Paktika Province near the Pakistan border.

Suddenly, they were ambushed.

From a nearby ridgeline, RPGs and small-arms fire rained down on the convoy. An RPG barely missed the lead vehicle, which carried platoon leader Lieutenant Billy Mariani and three others. His driver, Private First Class Cory Rambo, floored the accelerator and sped out of the line of fire. When Mariani learned that the Afghans' pickup was still stuck in the kill zone and receiving heavy fire, he and his comrades turned around, drove back into the perilous area, and helped evacuate the Afghans.

American machine gunners laid suppressing fire on the ridge-line while the mortar section shelled the enemy's positions. From behind hills and crags, still more bullets and RPGs ripped toward the soldiers. The Afghans' pickup was destroyed, and all the other vehicles took rounds.

The enemy then targeted the up-armored Humvee that was behind the pickup, bringing up the rear of the convoy. Three RPGs slammed into the vehicle, which held five soldiers. The first round exploded against the passenger-side door next to where Staff Sergeant Eric Wynn, 31, the truck commander, was sitting. No one was injured in the blast. The Americans' luck held when the second RPG hit the front of the Humvee, but didn't blow up.

The third one, however, crashed through the window in front of Wynn and sideswiped his face, slicing off the tip of his nose and part of his upper lip. It then struck Private First Class Channing Moss, who was behind and above him, perched in a gunner's sling. Facing the rear, Moss was firing the MK19 grenade launcher from the Humvee's turret when the RPG bored into the left side of his hip, tore through his lower abdomen, and lodged deep inside his body. The tip of the device stopped just short of breaking through the skin on Moss's upper right thigh. Incredibly, this RPG didn't explode, either.

About three feet long, an RPG travels at the speed of a bullet. At the front end is the warhead — a large grenade originally designed to strike tanks and armored vehicles, but now used in all combat situations, especially ambushes. The warhead sits on a shaft that contains a small rocket engine, fuel, and tail fins that pop up after the RPG is fired to stabilize its flight and guide it to the target.

Moss stopped firing his weapon. He smelled smoke and looked down at his stomach. He discovered that what was smoking was his wound from the RPG that was partially burrowed inside of him, its stabilizer fins jutting out his left side. Only then did it occur to him that he had been hit, that he was impaled by an explosive rocket — and that he would probably blow up any second.

Despite blood gushing from what was left of his nose and upper lip, Wynn radioed Mariani, told him what had happened, then held Moss's hand, offering him all the comfort he could under the deadly circumstances.

Fortunately, Moss's best friend, Specialist Jared "Doc" Angell, the platoon medic, was riding in the same Humvee. With bullets pounding the vehicle, Angell helped Moss off his perch and laid him down in the backseat. Using all the gauze and bandages he had, the medic tried to stop the bleeding. He gave Moss a shot of morphine to dull the pain and secured the RPG to the body, hoping that would prevent an explosion from too much movement. The medic was desperately trying to buy Moss enough time to get him to surgery.

Meanwhile, Specialist Andrew Vernon manned Moss's MK19 as the driver, Specialist Matthew Savoie, maneuvered the vehicle out of the kill zone. Mariani then radioed for medevac to come for the casualties — Moss, Wynn, and two wounded Afghans. Mariani deliberately did not mention the deadly RPG lodged in Moss. He knew that taking live ordnance aboard a medevac helicopter was against army regulations, even if it was an RPG stuck in the side of a soldier who was fighting for his life. Mariani didn't want to take the chance that permission would be denied to transport Moss.

As gunfire echoed nearby, Angell laid Moss on the dusty ground. "Please help me!" Moss cried out, thrashing in pain.

The medic was aware that any sudden movement could cause a typical RPG to explode, killing or maiming anyone within a 30-foot radius. But he remained by Moss's side, trying to calm him. "Hold on, Channing. Hold on. I'm going to do everything I can for you."

"Don't let them sandbag me!" Moss pleaded. He had become UXO — unexploded ordnance in military lingo — and was dangerous to himself and anyone around him. Moss was afraid that someone might move him behind a mound of sandbags a safe distance from the others and just let him bleed until he died.

When the firefight quieted down, Mariani hustled over to check on Moss as Angell continued to work on him. Trying not to wince at the sight of the lodged RPG, Mariani grabbed the soldier's hand and said, "Hey, buddy, we're going to get you out of here."

"I think I'm dying," Moss moaned. Barely five months out of basic training, the 23-year-old private feared he would never see his pregnant wife, Lorena, and two-year-old daughter, Yulina, who were back in his hometown of Gainesville, Georgia. "I don't want to die out here."

"That's not going to happen," Angell vowed. "Not on my watch."

Word reached Forward Operating Base (FOB) Salerno that four soldiers were seriously wounded and needed to be evacuated. Chief Warrant Officer 2 Jorge Correa, commander of a four-man Blackhawk medevac crew from the 159th Medical Company, prepared to take off. But his helicopter was held up for 15 minutes because Mariani's platoon was still engaged in combat. The area was simply too "hot" for the aircraft to land. After the chopper was given permission to go, Correa told his crew, "I don't know what to expect when we get there, so lock and load." They readied their weapons for combat.

Ten minutes later, the Blackhawk neared the battle scene where the airmen saw heavy smoke billowing from the burning pickup and soldiers running to different positions, still firing at the enemy. With an Apache attack helicopter in front to provide cover, Correa and his copilot, Chief Warrant Officer 1 Jeremy Smith, set their chopper down on a roadway a few yards from the plume of a smoke grenade that marked the landing zone. Specialist John Collier, the airborne medic, jumped out and dashed toward the wounded men.

Collier found an Afghan soldier whose hands were blown off and another who was missing the back of his scalp from an enemy round. The medic checked what was remaining of Wynn's nose and upper lip. Next, Collier moved over to Moss, who appeared at first glance to have a dislocated hip and some sort of pipe sticking out. Then it dawned on Collier what it really was.

The medic rushed back to the Blackhawk and shouted to Correa, "There's a live RPG stuck in the side of a soldier, and he's still alive!"

"If we take him with us," said Correa, "we'll be bringing live ordnance aboard as well, and that is against regulations."

"I know. But if we don't get this guy to the hospital right away, he's going to die."

Correa nodded. As far as he was concerned, forget the regulations if it meant taking a chance on saving a soldier's life. But he felt an obligation to brief his entire crew of the risks involved. So he explained to the men the danger they faced: The RPG could explode, blowing the helicopter, the crew, and the wounded out of the sky. "Are you guys comfortable with this?" he asked them. To a man, and without any hesitation, they all agreed to take Moss.

"Let's just do our job and get him to the hospital," declared Staff Sergeant Christian Roberts, the crew chief. "We are not going to leave a U.S. soldier to die in the middle of Afghanistan."

Pushing aside their concerns for personal safety, the crew loaded the casualties into the helicopter. Because it was so crowded, two airmen gave up their seats to two of the wounded. Moss and the other casualty were each laid on a stretcher on the floor, with Moss loaded last so he could be the first one removed from the chopper.

After the Blackhawk lifted off, the pilots pushed its speed to the max and headed for the nearest medical facility about 20 miles away. During the short flight, some of the crewmen wondered whether Moss would survive. It had been more than 60 minutes since he was hit, which meant he was past the so-called "golden hour" of survival.

Correa and Roberts, veterans who had previously flown medical evacuation missions in Iraq, assumed they had seen it all by the time they were deployed to Afghanistan. But they never thought that one day they would be flying with a patient who was impaled with an RPG.

Major John Oh, 35, the army general surgeon on duty with 759th Forward Surgical Team (FST), Task Force Med at Orgun-E FOB, was waiting for the Blackhawk to arrive at his BAS, which was once a former goat shed. Tucked 7,000 feet up a mountain, it was often the first stop for injured soldiers evacuated from combat in the area. The FST's job was to perform surgery, if necessary, stabilize the patients, and prepare them for transport to the better-equipped combat-support hospital at Bagram Air Base near Kabul.

The medevac crewmen had alerted Oh of the four casualties, including the "urgent surgical." But the airmen did to Oh what platoon leader Billy Mariani did to them — they failed to mention the RPG. They kept mum on that crucial fact because they, like Mariani, feared army regulations wouldn't allow for swift treatment of Moss.

When the Blackhawk landed, Moss, who was barely alive, was rushed into the aid station. Meanwhile, Major Kevin Kirk, an orthopedic surgeon, assessed the other casualties. Because the facility had only one operating table, Kirk determined that the medevac crew could transport the three wounded soldiers to Bagram. He knew that as a critical trauma patient, Moss would take up all of the FST's resources.

It still wasn't apparent just how dangerous the situation was until Oh and his team began cutting away Moss's combat uniform and unraveling the gauze bandages. When they saw the tail fin of the RPG sticking out of him, Oh yelled, "Unexploded round! Everybody get out!"

Oh and his team got into their Kevlar body armor and put on their surgical scrubs and ballistic helmets. The surgeon studied the RPG, then looked into Moss's eyes, which shifted from a blank stare as he neared unconsciousness to a pleading gaze as he struggled to live. "I . . . can't . . . breathe," the soldier whispered with great effort.

Oh faced the same dilemma that confronted Correa, the Blackhawk pilot: Should he risk his life and those of his team in order to save the life of a wounded soldier? It was his call alone to make.

If we don't do something right away, he's going to die, Oh thought. *I can't let that happen. He's made it this far, so there's no way we can give up now.*

"We have to save this guy," Oh declared. "I need volunteers."

Everyone raised his hand. He selected his volunteers: Major Kevin Kirk; Lieutenant Colonel William Brock, a certified nurse anesthetist; Specialist Michael Rodriguez, OR technician; Captain Elizabeth Greiser, OR nurse; and Captain Jeffery Robbins, executive officer. Before they began to treat Moss, Oh called in a two-man team from Explosive Ordnance Disposal (EOD), Sergeant First Class Dan Brown and Specialist Emmanual Christian of 759th Ordnance Company. Normally, the two were outside the wire, defusing roadside bombs, but on this day they had remained on base.

When Brown arrived at the aid station, Oh told him, "You need to figure out what we can do about this thing and how likely it is to go off."

"If this RPG still has a warhead on it and it explodes, you'll be dead before the roof caves in," Brown said bluntly. "We won't know how dangerous it is, though, until we can get an X-ray of him. In the meantime, don't shake him or move him, because it's an unstable situation."

The medical team slipped a breathing tube down Moss's throat and began intubating him. Just then the monitoring equipment sounded an alarm, indicating Moss's blood pressure had plunged and his heart had stopped beating.

Oh knew that if he attempted CPR, the chest compressions would cause Moss's body to move, which could trigger the RPG. The surgeon quickly put in an IV line and started giving him a blood transfusion and a shot of epinephrine, a heart-stimulating medication. Those actions kick-started Moss's heart and brought up his blood pressure to an acceptable level. There would be no need for chest compression.

I've never been more scared in my life, Oh thought. *This is terrifying.* As he took a couple of deep breaths to soothe himself, he felt as though he was reevaluating his whole life in a microsecond.

Born in Seoul, South Korea, Oh was four when he and his parents immigrated to the United States, where he grew up in Beltsville, Maryland, and became a naturalized citizen. He went to West Point, earned an army scholarship to New York Medical College, did his residency in general surgery at Fort Bliss, Texas, and was deployed overseas, eventually arriving in Afghanistan on Thanksgiving Day 2005.

Now here he was four months later trying to save a life that, with one wrong move, could end up costing his own life and those of his comrades and patient.

Oh decided to give Moss a paralytic drug that would keep him from thrashing so they could take an X-ray. The surgeon had a choice to make: One drug works quickly but can cause the muscles to go into spasms before they relax. The other drug takes much longer to work but it doesn't cause spasms. Because time was crucial, Oh injected the faster drug. When Moss's body began to shake, everyone in the room wondered if they were about to blow up. *I should have used the other drug,* Oh thought. *Will the spasms make the RPG go off?*

A sense of relief enveloped the room when Moss stopped twitching. But the tension began to rise when the portable X-ray machine failed twice to take clear pictures. It finally worked the third time. When Brown, the explosives expert, studied the image, he said, "Good news. The X-ray shows that the fuse and warhead, which are the deadliest part of the RPG, are not inside Moss. Most likely they broke off when the RPG struck the windshield of the Humvee before it penetrated Moss."

"Great," said Oh. "Now we can relax."

"Not exactly," Brown replied. He explained that the rest of the RPG that was inside Moss contained a detonator, the small explosive charge that was supposed to set off the warhead.

"The detonator is still attached to the fuel rod that's in his abdomen, and it's sensitive to electric current," Brown warned. "The potential for blowing up is less without the warhead, but it could still explode at any time. And if it does, it definitely will kill your patient and take off your fingers and ruin your career, not to mention cause serious damage to the hands and limbs of everyone in this room. This remains a grave, unstable situation."

Moss was still bleeding from the gaping hole in his pelvis.

"He's hemorrhaging," Oh announced. "We can't wait any longer. We have to take him to OR."

When they wheeled Moss into the tiny operating room next door, Oh took off his flak vest because it was too bulky for him to perform surgery. He discarded his helmet, too, so he could use his headlamp. The surgeon was now completely defenseless against any kind of explosion.

Before starting the operation, he gave his volunteers the opportunity to back out. "You do understand what's going on here and how dangerous this situation is, right?" he said. "You could die. You can leave now if you want." No one moved. They didn't say a word.

"I take that to mean yes. Okay, then. This thing is coming out of him no matter what. There's no way we're going to let him die. It just can't happen."

Brown's EOD partner, Specialist Christian, insisted on staying in the OR so he could record the surgery with his digital camera. "I need to record this because you're not likely to ever see this again," he told the medical team.

Oh needed to assess the damage to Moss's abdomen and study the path of the RPG. Fighting his own apprehension, the surgeon picked up his scalpel, which had an electric charge that cauterizes (burns) the wound to prevent infection while cutting. *Will this set off the detonator?* he wondered. *If so, these will be the last people I'm ever going to see.* He cleared his throat and told the volunteers, "If this thing goes off, I just want all of you to know that it's been great working with you."

In one of the most delicate incisions of his life, Oh cut over the right thigh by the hip, which was the opposite side of the

RPG's entry point. His knife sliced just a fraction of an inch from the front of the projectile. "I can see the tip," said the surgeon.

"Yeah, you're close enough so that if it blows up, you might lose your fingers," said Brown.

"That's a comforting thought."

When Moss's abdomen was opened, Oh saw that the soldier's intestines were shredded, his pelvic bone was crushed, and he had lost a lot of blood. However, his spine and major organs had not been disturbed, although the RPG was lying right below the aorta, the main artery from the heart to the lower part of the body.

Oh also saw that the RPG had struck the soldier's utility belt as it entered his pelvis and dragged dirt, the belt, and a piece of uniform all the way across his abdomen, making the wound ripe for infection.

Now it was time to remove the RPG. Oh clutched the device but couldn't shove it back the way it had come in. The surgical team had to figure out another approach to extract the RPG from Moss's body without killing him or setting off the detonator. The team decided the device would have to be pulled through his right side rather than tugging the detonator across the abdominal cavity and out through the entry point. To deal with the RPG's tail fins that were still protruding from Moss's left hip, Brown got a hacksaw and said, "This is the only way we'll get it out."

"Do what you have to do," said Oh.

Wearing his flak jacket, Brown kneeled under the surgical sheet and, in a gentle but steady motion, began sawing off the fins while Oh held the device with a firm grip. As an EOD technician, Brown had worked in places like Bosnia, defusing live ordnance from bodies in graves. But he had never dealt with trying to remove an explosive from a live patient before.

No one said a word in the OR while Brown sawed. Oh glanced around the room and wondered if his eyes were as wide and frightened as those of his volunteers.

When the fins were cut off, the team began the next delicate step. Brown stepped to the other side of Moss's body and crouched down so he was eye level with the tip of the RPG. He slowly squeezed his hands around the blood-covered projectile. With the dangerous detonator pointed directly at his chest, Brown gently eased it across Moss's open abdominal cavity, close to his beating heart, while the surgeons cut away around it. Oh helped guide the device while Kirk pinched off Moss's aorta to preserve blood flow to his head, heart, and vital organs. The soldier's belt still clung to the RPG.

"Okay, there's the belt buckle," said Brown. "It's coming. Keep feeding it — you feed it and I'll hold it," Brown told Oh, who continued to cut around the RPG. Ever so slowly and carefully, they maneuvered the device through Moss's body.

"Almost there," Oh told Brown. "About three more inches."

And then: "We're clear!" Brown announced. "We're clear!"

"All right!"

Cradling the RPG like a baby, Brown rushed outside and placed it into a sandbagged bunker where he wrapped it in C-4 explosives and safely blew it up in a thunderous roar heard throughout the base. That was when the emotional impact of the ordeal finally hit Brown. His body began to quiver and his legs went limp. He slid to the ground and wept.

Oh and his team were so intent on saving Moss's life that

they couldn't calm down after the RPG's removal. Although they were glad it was out of him, they had another critical issue to deal with: Moss was still bleeding to death. Totally focused and with a minimum of talking, the surgical team went into overdrive to curb the hemorrhaging, do an emergency repair of his intestines, and clean up the contamination caused by the RPG.

Two and a half hours after Moss was brought to the BAS, the surgical team had done all it could for him. He was still alive after the operation. Unconscious and remaining in critical condition, he was transported by helicopter to Bagram.

As the relieved surgeon and volunteers watched the chopper take off, Oh thanked everybody. "You guys did a great job," he told them. "You should feel real good about what you've done. We accomplished something today that we'll probably never experience again. And, more importantly, we put our lives on the line to save a soldier."

Channing Moss underwent another operation at Bagram before he was flown the next day to the army's Landstuhl Regional Medical Center in Germany. When he regained consciousness there, his first words were, "Am I alive?"

Five days after he was impaled by the RPG, Moss, who was missing two-thirds of his intestines and couldn't walk, was transported to Walter Reed Army Medical Center in Bethesda, Maryland, where he amazed surgeons with his steady recovery.

Three months after the attack, he attended the birth of his second daughter, Ariana.

Moss, who was promoted to specialist, was told he would be given a Purple Heart for his wounds in combat. But he didn't want to receive it in his hospital room. It was important for him to walk across the stage to accept it. After four major surgeries and months of grueling physical therapy, he moved from a hospital bed to a wheelchair to a walker to a cane. "I wanted to walk and get my medal and let everyone know I fought hard," Moss told reporters after receiving his medal. "They say 'Army Strong' and I wanted to be an example of that, and I was. So I stood up, I walked over there and got my medal."

After receiving the Purple Heart, Moss, who is now medically discharged from the service, underwent two more major operations and countless other medical procedures. Physical therapy became a part of his daily routine.

The former infantryman, who had joined the army to help give his family a better life, said he knows he's alive because of his fellow soldiers. "I don't think there has been a day that I haven't thought about them, that I haven't prayed for them," he said. "They saved my life."

For his part in risking his own life to keep Moss alive under perilous conditions, Major John Oh received the Soldier's Medal at the Carl R. Darnall Army Medical Center in Fort Hood, Texas, in 2007. The medal is the military's highest decoration for heroism not involving actual combat with an enemy force.

Dr. Oh said he had ignored army regulations in this case "because I felt Channing Moss had a chance to make it." He added, "For me to do this once, it's not that heroic. The soldiers who go outside the wire and put their lives at risk every day, that's heroic."

Lieutenant Colonel William Brock and Major Kevin Kirk each

earned an Army Commendation Medal with Valor for assisting Dr. Oh.

Staff Sergeant Eric Wynn, the truck commander whose face was seriously injured from the incoming RPG that slammed into Moss, received a Purple Heart. It took three operations to repair his nose and upper lip.

Awarded an Air Medal with Valor were medevac pilot Jorge Correa, who was promoted to Chief Warrant Officer 3, and flight medic John Collier, who was promoted to Sergeant. Also receiving Air Medals were copilot Jeremy Smith, who was promoted to Chief Warrant Officer 2, and Staff Sergeant Christian Roberts, the crew chief.

Field medic Jared Angell, who was promoted to Sergeant, and Sergeant First Class Dan Brown, the explosives expert, were each awarded the Bronze Star with Valor. Brown told reporters that everyone who risked his life for Moss did so because "he was an American, he was a solider, he was a brother, and he was one of us." Brown added, "Nothing was going to stop us from doing what we knew we had to do. We knew we did right. In that screwed-up world over there, we did something right."

Glossary

A-10 Warthog: a fixed-wing, single-seat, twin-engine air force jet plane designed for close air support; officially called an A-10 Thunderbolt, but more commonly called Warthog or Hog

AC-130 gunship: a fixed-wing, heavily armed air force attack aircraft powered by four turboprops and manned by a crew of 12

adrenaline: a hormone produced by the body that prepares the individual to deal with stress

AK-47: an enemy automatic assault rifle, originally manufactured in the former Soviet Union

ANA: Afghan National Army

ANP: Afghan National Police

AT4: a portable one-shot antitank weapon

battalion: a military unit usually consisting of from 500 to 1,500 persons in two to six companies and a headquarters

battle aid station (BAS): a medical unit close to combat that treats the wounded before they are taken to a hospital

battle buddies: pairs of soldiers who stick together and look out for each other during combat

bomb damage assessment (BDA): an estimate from ground forces of the damage inflicted on a close enemy target by gunships and bombs; also known as battle damage assessment

C-4: a military plastic explosive easily formed, like modeling clay, into any desired shape

cache: a hiding place where weapons and ammunition are stored

cell leader: a militant in charge of a cell—one of many small groups that make up a terrorist organization—and normally is the only one who communicates with higher-ups or other cells

cleared hot: a term giving pilots the approval to engage a target and/or release bombs

close air support: helicopters and/or attack planes that shoot at or bomb hostile forces that are near friendly forces

company: a military unit usually consisting of three to five platoons

corpsman: a medically trained enlisted naval person assigned to provide battlefield medical care to Marines or sailors

danger close: when friendly troops are within 600 meters of an artillery target

deployment: the assignment of military personnel to a tour of duty

engage: attack

escalation of force: a military procedure in which appropriate levels of action are taken against a potential threat. Verbal commands are issued first; deadly force is used only as a last resort.

F-14 Tomcat: a supersonic, twin-engine, two-seat navy fighter jet

F-16 Fighting Falcon: a supersonic, single-engine, single-pilot air force fighter jet; also known as the Viper because it resembles a cobra

firefight: a battle between ground forces using guns, grenades, and other fired weapons

flak jacket: a vest made of bullet-resistant Kevlar and nylon, designed to stop fragments from grenades, rockets, and bullets; also called body armor

forward air controller: a person who coordinates air strikes

forward operating base (FOB): a small, secure, sometimes temporary base typically closer to combat situations than the main operating base

frag (or fragmentation) grenade: an antipersonnel weapon designed to spread shrapnel upon exploding

friendly fire: an attack, bombing, or shooting that was meant to kill the enemy but accidentally injured or killed one or more American or allied troops or innocent civilians

Green Beret: a member of the U.S. Army Special Forces

gunship: an armed attack aircraft

HH-60 Pave Hawk: an air force combat search-and-rescue helicopter

Humvee: a wide-bodied, all-terrain four-wheel-drive truck

IED: an improvised explosive device typically known as a roadside bomb

insurgent: a person who takes part in an armed rebellion; a militant

IV: short for intravenous; a fluid drip administered directly into a vein

kill zone: an area in a battle where the enemy hopes to kill the most soldiers

leatherneck: slang for Marine

M4: a lightweight, short-barreled military carbine assault rifle

M9: semiautomatic 9-mm pistol

M16: the most widely used military automatic assault rifle

M203: a single-shot grenade launcher that attaches to the M16 or M4 carbine

M240B: a standard-infantry, medium-sized machine gun

M249: a light machine gun typically used as a squad automatic weapon

M72 LAW: a portable, one-shot, unguided light antitank weapon

magazine: a container holding rounds of ammunition that is inserted into a weapon

medevac: a term for medical evacuation; a mission flown by helicopters to remove wounded personnel from a battle area

militant: a person who takes part in an armed rebellion; an insurgent

MK19: a belt-fed automatic 40-mm grenade launcher

morphine: a strong painkiller

mortar: a muzzle-loading, high-angle gun with a short barrel that fires shells at high elevations for a short range

mosque: a Muslim house of worship

mullah: a Muslim male trained in Islam who is a religious teacher or leader

neutralized: military slang for killed

outside the wire: beyond the safety of the perimeter; on patrol

perimeter: the guarded boundary that forms the outer limits of a military force's position

PKM: a general-purpose machine gun manufactured in Russia

platoon: a small military unit typically consisting of three squads of between 20 and 30 persons per squad

Purple Heart: a U.S. military decoration awarded to members of the armed forces who have been wounded or killed in action

quick reaction force (QRF): a small military group that is poised to respond on short notice, typically less than fifteen minutes, to a combat situation

radio traffic: the amount of activity broadcast over a communications system

recon: short for doing a reconnaissance, an exploration or examination of an area to gather military information

RPG: a rocket-propelled grenade launched from a shoulder-fired portable weapon

RPK: a handheld light machine gun, originally manufactured in the former Soviet Union

rules of engagement: regulations concerning the limitations and circumstances of when, where, and how forces can attack the enemy

SAW: squad automatic weapon, typically an M249 light machine gun

shrapnel: fragments from an exploded mine, bomb, or shell

Special Forces: an elite unit of the U.S. Army trained for unconventional warfare, reconnaissance, search and rescue, and counterterrorism; known as the Green Berets

suppressive fire: a flurry of rounds directed at the enemy to keep them pinned down, preventing them from shooting at moving targets; also called cover fire

troops in contact: combat against an enemy force

tour or tour of duty: a period of time spent assigned to service in a foreign country

tracer round: a bullet filled with a flare that burns bright, allowing the shooter to get a better aim on a moving target

turret: a self-contained weapons platform housing guns on a vehicle and capable of rotation

UH-60 Blackhawk: four-bladed, twin-engine tactical transport helicopter

About the Author

Allan Zullo is the author of nearly 100 nonfiction books on subjects ranging from sports and the supernatural to history and animals.

He has introduced readers to the *Ten True Tales* series, gripping stories of extraordinary persons — many of them young people — who have met the challenges of dangerous, sometimes life-threatening, situations. Among the books in the series are *War Heroes: Voices from Iraq, World War II Heroes,* and *Teens at War.* In addition, he has authored three books about the real-life experiences of kids during the Holocaust — *Survivors: True Stories of Children in the Holocaust, Heroes of the Holocaust: True Stories of Rescues by Teens,* and *Escape: Children of the Holocaust.*

Allan, the grandfather of five and the father of two grown daughters, lives with his wife, Kathryn, on the side of a mountain near Asheville, North Carolina. To learn more about the author, visit his Web site at www.allanzullo.com.